Create Independent Learners

These Patricia Pavelka titles available from:

Crystal Springs Books — 1-800-924-9621

Making the Connection:
Learning Skills Through Literature (K-2)

Making the Connection:
Learning Skills Through Literature (3-6)

Creating and Managing Effective Centers & Themes (video)

For more information on attending a workshop with
Patricia Pavelka, or having her come to your school for an
inservice seminar, please contact:

The Society For Developmental Education
Ten Sharon Road
PO Box 577
Peterborough, NH 03458
1-800-924-9621

CREATE INDEPENDENT LEARNERS

Teacher-Tested Strategies
for ALL Ability Levels

by
Patricia Pavelka

Edited by
Diane Cherkerzian

Illustrated by
Susan Dunholter
Cynthia Dumas

Crystal Springs
BOOKS

Published by
Crystal Springs Books · Peterborough, NH
1-800-321-0401

Printed in the United States of America

Published by Crystal Springs Books
Ten Sharon Road
PO Box 500
Peterborough, NH 03458
1-800-321-0401
FAX: 1-800-337-9929

Publisher Cataloging-in-Publication Data

Pavelka, Patricia, 1959-.
      Create independent learners: teacher-tested strategies
for all ability levels / Patricia Pavelka ; edited by Diane
Cherkerzian ; illustrated by Susan Dunholter and Cynthia
Dumas.-1st. ed.
[159] p. : ill.: cm.
Summary : Ideas, strategies and hands-on activities for
teachers to use in all of the curriculum with students of all
ability levels, and to use to involve parents with their child's
education.
ISBN 1-884548-24-5
1. Learning-study and teaching. 2. Creative activities and
seat work. 3. Language Arts. I. Cherkerzian, Diane.
II. Dunholter, Susan, 1956— , ill. III. Dumas, Cynthia, 1949—, ill.
IV. Title.
370.15/ 23 -dc21   1999   CIP
LC Number: 99-72218

Editor: Diane Cherkerzian
Cover Design, Book Design and Illustrations: Susan Dunholter
Cover Illustrations, Illustrator: Cynthia Dumas

Publishing Manager: Lorraine Walker
Publishing Projects Coordinator: Meredith A. Reed

Rose Al Clara Tony Judy

Connie Oliver

Annette Kristi Theresa Connie

Ralph John Matthew

Paul Alisha Trish Cathi Carol

Eric Diana Melinda

Dana Leann

Pat Jonathan Sara Barry

Tom

Rich Janine Christine Jo-Ann

Matthew Michael Kevin

Dom Stacie Jack Tom John

Carla Laura

Tina Phyllis Sara Vinnie

Dedicated
to my
Family

Acknowledgements

Thank you to Richard LaPorta, my brother, for always believing in me and working by my side;

To Mom, my best friend, for taking over many of my responsibilities so I could complete this book;

To Lorraine Walker at Crystal Springs Books for her encouragement and confidence in me;

To Diane Cherkerzian, my talented editor, for her incredible ability to organize and keep me focused;

To Ken Mazur, my Mac Man, for always being available and for his patience;

To my colleagues and friends at SDE for their constant support and guidance;

And to Jim Grant, Irv Richardson, and Jay LaRoche for the many opportunities they have given me to touch the lives of teachers and children.

Contents

INTRODUCTION 11

Part 1: Foundations

Building Foundations for the Year 14
   Getting Yourself Ready 15

Organizational Strategies for Classroom Materials 16
   Organizational Time 17
      Organizational Time at the End of Each Day 17
      Have Students Set Up Organizational Time 17
      Student-Created Checklists 18
      Students Help Each Other 19
      Clean Desks Daily 19
      Places to Keep Checklists 20

   Organizing Papers 21
      Color Coding Subjects (for older students) 21
      Getting Supplies: Sample Letter to Parents 22
      Work Folders (for younger students) 23
      Home/School Connection: Notices & Papers 24
         Home/SchoolFolder (for younger students)
         Home/School Envelope
         ➥ Envelope Checklist 25
      Organizational Checklist Samples 26

Strategies to Help Students Organize Information and Make Connections 29
   Think Alouds 30
      What Are Think Alouds? 30
      Why Use Think Alouds? 30
      Modeling Think Alouds 30
      Teacher to Student 31
      Student to Student 31
      Think Aloud Cloud (for younger students) 32
      Bounce an Idea (for older students) 32
      ➥ Think Aloud Cloud 33
      🔍 Think Alouds 34

Student Interest and Motivation 36
   Becoming Team Players 37
      One Way Is Not the Best (for older students) 37
      "It's Not Fair!" (for younger students) 38
      It Takes Two 39
   Decision Making and Ownership 40
      In & Out Cans 40
      How to Make In and Out Cans 40
      Picking Volunteers 40
      Everyone Has a Chance 40
      Keeping Students Attentive 41
      Active Learners 41
   Inventories 42
      Reading Inventory 42
      ➥ Reading Inventory 44
      🔍 Reading Inventory 46

🔍 A Closer Look Page   ➥ A Reproducible Page

Interviews 48
    Interest Interview 48
    ➛ Interest Interview 49

Part 2: Strategies and Activities for Language Arts

Three Cueing Systems 52
    Prompting Language 53
        ⚲ Prompting Language 53
        Strategy Poster 54
        Strategy Cards 54
    Cloze Activities 55
        Individual Sentences 56
        Big Books and Post-It® Notes 55
        Morning Messages 56
    Decoding and Spelling with Pattern Words 57
        Pattern Word Wall 57
        Involve Your Students 58
        Organizing the Wall 58
        Putting Words on the Wall 58
        Choosing Words 59
        Teaching Students to Use the Wall 59
    Turning Skills Into Strategies 60
        Have-A-Go 60
            How to Use Have-A-Go Sheets 60
            Review Skills 61
            Guided Reading 61
            Writing Time 61
            Editing 62
            Assessment 62
            Inform Your Teaching 62
            ➛ Have-A-Go 63
    More Ways to Practice and Use Spelling Patterns and Rules 64
        Practice with Pattern Words 64
            Plastic Letters 64
            Rhyming Riddles 65
            Highlighting Tape 66
            Flipbooks 66
    Decoding and Spelling with Sight Words 67
        Sight Words 67
            A Separate Place 67
            Create Visuals 68
            Have-A-Go 68
    Look Cover Write Check 69
        Sight Words 69
            How to Use Look Cover Write Check (LCWC) 69
            ⚲ LCWC 70
            ⚲ LCWC 71
            ➛ LCWC 72
            Glue Words 73
            ⚲ Glue Words 74
    Pulling It All Together 75
        Traveling Strategy Folders 75

⚲ *A Closer Look Page*   ➛ *A Reproducible Page*

Managing Traveling Strategy Folders 75
Independent Reading 76
Success at Home and School 76
➥ Traveling Strategy Folder 77
Sustained Silent Reading(SSR) & Building Good Reading Habits 78
SSR 79
Before Reading 79
After Reading 79
Writing 80
Boxes and Arrows 80
➥ Boxes and Arrows 81
🔍 Writing (with younger students) 82
🔍 Writing (with older students) 84
➥ Character Development 86
➥ Setting Development 86

Part 3: Strategies & Activities Across the Curriculum

Strategies and Activities Across the Curriculum 90
Flipbooks 91
How to Make a Flipbook 91
🔍 Flipbooks: A Sample Four-Day Lesson Plan 92
Predictions 96
Sequencing 97
Step-by-Step 97
Word Problems 98
Descriptive Questions 99
🔍 Flipbooks 100
Vocabulary Development 102
Highlighting Tape 103
Reading and Writing 103
Print Concepts 103
Sight Words 103
Writing Difficulties 104
Play with Print 105
➥ Play with Print Cards 105
🔍 Highlighting Tape 106
Inferencing 107
It's Inbetween the Lines 107
Homework Helper 107
Previewing 108
Previewing Text (for older students) 108
Prepare for Tests 108
Picture and Word Walks (for younger students) 108
Webs 109
Sense Webs 110
➥ Sense Web 111
Question Webs 112
➥ Question Web 113
Student Generated Webs 114
Transition from Webs 117
Help Students Transfer from Webs to Writing 117
🔍 Transition from Webs 118

🔍 A Closer Look Page   ➥ A Reproducible Page

Scripts 120
    Math Scripts 120
    Creating a Script 120
    Make a Script Book 121
    Make a Script Folder 121
    ⌕ Scripts 122
Graphic Organizers and Structured Overviews 124
    Organize Your Goals 124
    How Students Use the Organizers 126
    A List of Vocabulary and Information 127
Using These Activities and Strategies Within the
Context of a Diverse Classroom 128
    Let Students Show What They Know 129
        ⌕ Show What You Know 130
You're Never at a Dead End 132
    Make a Signpost 133

Part 4: Home-School Connection

Parents as Partners 136
    Reading 137
        Comprehension and Language Development 138
    Homework Helpers 139
        Chunking Homework 139
        Chunk a Task into Smaller Parts 139
        Managing Many Assignments 139
        ➼ Letter to Parents 140
        ➼ Chunking Homework Worksheet 141
        Calendar of Assignments and Responsibilities 142
    Spelling Strategy Folder 143
        ➼ Letter to Parents 144
        Helping Children Understand New Information 146
        Quick Books 146
        ➼ Letter to Parents: How to Make a Quick Book 147
    Parent Workshops 148
        Tips 148
        Publicity 149
        ⌕ Parent Workshops 150
        ➼ Letter to Parents: Writing at Home 152
        ⌕ Writing at Home 153
        ➼ Letter to Parents: Reading at Home 154

RESOURCES: Suggested Professional Reading 155

⌕ A Closer Look Page   ➼ A Reproducible Page

Introduction

As educators, the ultimate goal for all of our students is that they begin to apply strategies on their own; that they learn how to be independent, strategic, successful learners. Students need to know exactly what to do when learning gets difficult.

This book is full of activities, strategies, and ideas to help students of all learning abilities become independent learners.

Please do not think of anything in this book as an addition to your curriculum. Your curriculum is already packed. You have enough to teach and be accountable for without adding to the list. The suggestions in this book are meant to help you deliver your curriculum, not add to it. The recommendations in this book can be implemented immediately. You will not have to spend hours making and buying new things. Tie all the ideas here to your specific students, materials, and skills you are accountable for teaching.

This book is divided into four parts.

Foundations

Part 1 deals with building foundations. Foundations include classroom routines and methods of organization, as well as knowing what motivates and interests your students. Foundations support everything that we build on top. If foundations are solid and strong, we can build high and wide. And the building for us is students' achievement across all curriculum areas.

Strategies and Activities for Language Arts

Part 2 gives a repertoire of ideas and suggestions to help students in the language arts area. Areas that are addressed include: using the three cueing systems, spelling and decoding, pattern words, sight words, and writing.

Strategies Across the Curriculum

Part 3 focuses on five specific activities and strategies to help students become independent, strategic, successful learners across the curriculum. This section also shows how to manage and apply these ideas within the contexts of your diverse classrooms.

Home/School Connection

Part 4 explores how to build a home/school connection. There are specific ideas and activities that parents can do at home with children when they are facing difficult tasks. There is information about how to set up parent workshops and informational evenings. Reproducible parent letters are also included.

Special Features

A Closer Look: A Real Life Classroom Example

All of the ideas and strategies in this book have been used in my classroom or other colleagues' classrooms. Throughout this book is a feature called *A Closer Look: A Real Life Classroom Example*. These are examples of a strategy or idea being applied and utilized in a real classroom with actual students. After reading about an idea or activity in this book, *A Closer Look* allows you to glimpse into a classroom and hear dialogue and see the strategy being used successfully.

Younger/Older

Throughout the book I will refer to *younger students* and *older students*. Activities found next to *younger students* work well with children in grades 1 and 2. Activities found next to *older students* work well with children in grades 3 through 5. These are only suggestions! You may find that an activity marked for younger children suits the needs of your older students. On the other hand, you might teach first grade and find an older suggestion will work better for you and your students.

Part 1
Foundations

Building Foundations
for the Year

At the start of each school year I was so excited about beginning my reading program, starting my writing workshop, having my students keep science journals, passing out new books, etc., that little was done to thoughtfully establish the foundations for successful, independent learning in my classroom.

Time was not taken to help students learn how to organize themselves and their work. They were not taught how to be strategic learners. We just took off and went into the academics. I was very aware of the large curriculum that needed to be completed throughout the year, but less aware of my students' interests and attitudes. So off we would go into the academics and leave the foundation to become solid and strong by itself — which of course it never did.

As the year progressed, and work became increasingly difficult, struggling students began falling further and further behind and problems arose. Students became disorganized and frustrated. There was always a line at my desk. They couldn't find their papers and pencils. They were at dead ends with nowhere to go. Students were not supporting each other—either they just gave their friends the answers or they became competitive. The foundation that was supposed to support and hold our learning together was weak and crumbling because it was not carefully constructed.

There are two foundational issues that are essential in creating an effective classroom. They are:

- **Organization:** This includes ways to help students organize their physical classroom materials and ways to help students meaningfully organize the information they are learning.

- **Student Interest and Motivation:** This includes helping students learn to be collaborators, not competitors, and finding out what their interests are to better inform our teaching.

Getting Yourself Ready

Do you remember the first time you learned how to do something new? You may have been very excited to begin, but as you started it wasn't as easy as you thought. Something you thought would take a day to complete or a day to become an expert at just didn't happen. It felt awkward and uncomfortable. You might have even considered never trying it again. But after some practice it became quicker, easier, and you felt very successful.

The first couple of times you introduce and try the following strategies you might feel like you're in the middle of a disaster! It takes five times longer than you had planned, students seem more confused now than before, and you think:

"I'll never do this again. Just get me through the next period."

Give these strategies time to "hum." Soon it will be smooth and easy. You and your students will be able to do them with little thought.

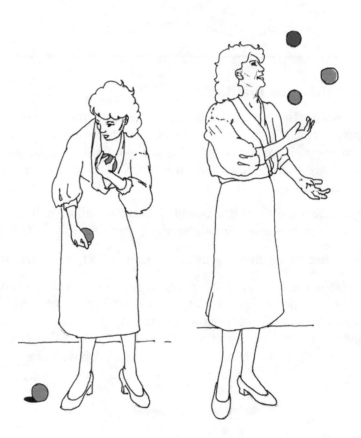

Organizational Strategies
to Help Students Organize Classroom Materials

Does this look familiar?

Students often have an extremely difficult time with organization: losing papers, misplacing pencils, etc. Students face more and more challenges in organizing themselves the older they get. If we can start helping them in their younger years, then by the time they are in the sixth grade and have five different teachers, they will have a number of strategies to fall back on.

As a classroom teacher I would constantly tell myself that I needed to stop 5-10 minutes before the day was over to help students get organized. This happened maybe twice a week.

The other three days it was . . . ***"Let's go, the buses are here!"***

Students raced around the room to get ready to board the buses for home. When the dust cleared, my younger students left their hats, coats, mittens, backpacks and lunchboxes all over the room. My older students left their homework and notices on their desks or on the floor. Students were setting themselves up for failure. They left without the things they needed to begin the following day on a positive note.

What happens at the end of the day today significantly impacts how tomorrow will begin.

Organizational Time at the End of the Day

How can an organizational time be set up so it is consistent each day? The first step is to have students own the organizational time. We all know that when we are told what to do and how to do it, our "buy in" or motivation is not high. Yet when we are asked to be a part of the decision making process and end goals, our motivation and interest immediately grow. Also, when we tell our students to remind us they never let us forget.

 ## Have Students Set Up the Organizational Time

One of the biggest mistakes I made in my teaching career was doing too much outside of school, before or after school, without my students. I would create and set up activities, organize the day, and make bulletin boards and displays without them. My students didn't take part in setting up the plan or activity and so there was no ownership on their part. Immediately their motivation and interest decreased. The more students are involved from the beginning, the more effective and efficient the strategy, activity or idea becomes.

Some classrooms named the organizational time:

OT Organizational Time

TOOT Time Out Organizational Time

SOS Super Organized Students

A first grade teacher in Brookline, MA shared these ideas:

GRIN Get Right Into Neatness

CUT Clean Up Time

REST Review Everything and Save Time

A third and fourth grade teacher in Nashua, NH shared these ideas:

OOT Official Organizational Time

BOOT Buddy Official Organizational Time

Student-Created Checklists

Students also set up an organizational checklist that needs to be completed at the end of each day. (Sample checklists are found on pages 26-28.) First brainstorm what things need to be done at the end of the day. The first list your students come up with may be 20 items long. Revise the list by adding and deleting, finally developing a checklist that students created. The checklist can be put on a chart for all students to see and use, but some students may need more support. For example, students often look up at a chart and lose their place. Also, by the time they look down from the chart, they forget what they just read. Some might have difficulty reading it from where they are sitting. Students find it helpful to have their own copy.

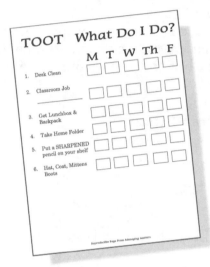

The sample checklist found on page 26 has been used with **younger children** who have one primary teacher and little homework. The line under Classroom Job is used to write down the child's job for the week.

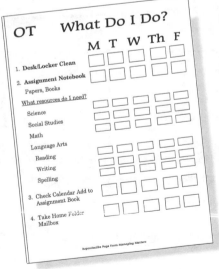

The sample checklist found on page 27 has been used with **older children** who may have more than one teacher and a number of different homework assignments. Many times students have the homework or assignment written down in their assignment notebook, but then forget to take home the resources needed to complete the work. This checklist helps students make sure they have all the materials they will need when they leave school.

Students Help Each Other

Students are paired for organizational time: a disorganized student with an organized partner. The student who has no difficulty with organization usually completes the checklist in minutes and then goes to his disorganized partner. The checklist shows students how to help each other. They will follow the boxes together, looking at what needs to be done next. The organized student may read from the list as his partner does his own work. This way one student is not doing the work for the other.

Clean Desks Daily

Notice on the sample checklists that Desk Clean is the first item to complete. Desk cleans are usually done on Friday afternoons. There is so much *STUFF* in the desks that when students take it all out you can't see the floor! At that point they don't even know where to begin. There are students who, when told to clean their desks, really don't know what to do. They become paper shufflers and just move papers and books around. And then when told to finish up they shove everything back in their desk!

By having a desk clean every day, it takes only minutes to clean. The task becomes manageable. It is more of a straightening up then a full-fledged clean. A sample Desk Clean checklist is found on page 28.

DESK CLEAN

M T W Th F

1. Take everything out
2. Put back Books
3. Pile the loose Papers
4. Put loose papers in colored folders
5. Put colored folders back in desk
6. Put back pencils, markers, etc.
7. Bring everything else up to your teacher

Places to keep checklists so they don't get lost.

Desks

Punch a hole in the top of the organizational paper and tie a piece of yarn to it. The yarn can then be taped to the side or front of each child's desk. At the end of the day students pull up the paper and place it right on top of their desk.

After they complete the tasks, their paper is just dropped back down. Each Friday students pull off their old sheet and tie on a new one. Another idea would be to laminate the sheets so students could use the same one all year.

Pocket Folders

Students each have a pocket folder titled: It Never Leaves My Desk. They decorate their folder and have to put something else on it, in addition to the title, to help them remember that it doesn't leave the desk. The organizational sheets are kept in the folder.

Notebooks

Older students who have a number of different teachers throughout the day can use a three-ring binder that travels with them to each class. The organizational sheets are kept inside the binder. Usually organizational time is done at the end of each period.

A Place for Papers

Papers seem to pose one of the biggest problems for students who struggle with organization. They often just shove their papers in their desks. Important ones never make it home or never get completed or corrected.

Organizing Papers

Color-Coding Subjects (for older students)

Color coding subjects helps all students to be extremely organized with their papers. We have a rule in our classroom: no papers in the desks. All papers must be in a folder. Color coding subject areas throughout the whole school ensures continuity among the grades. Assign a color to each subject area. Depending on your grade level, students will need a pocket folder and/or a spiral notebook in each of the colors. These pocket folders ensure that papers will not be just shoved in the desks.

Display the subjects and their corresponding colors in the classroom for students to refer to.

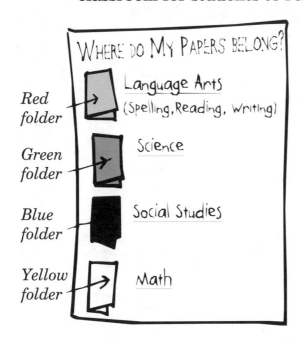

Red folder

Green folder

Blue folder

Yellow folder

Taping an index card with this information onto students' desks is also helpful.

This color coding system also helps when students go from teacher to teacher, or classroom to classroom. To make sure students have the correct books and materials, teachers can refer to the colors: "Everyone needs to take their red notebooks and red pocket folders." You can look at the line of students and immediately see who is missing something or who might have the wrong books and materials.

Foundations

Getting Supplies: A Sample Letter to Parents

The following is a sample letter written to parents. This letter goes home with students on the last day of school in June.

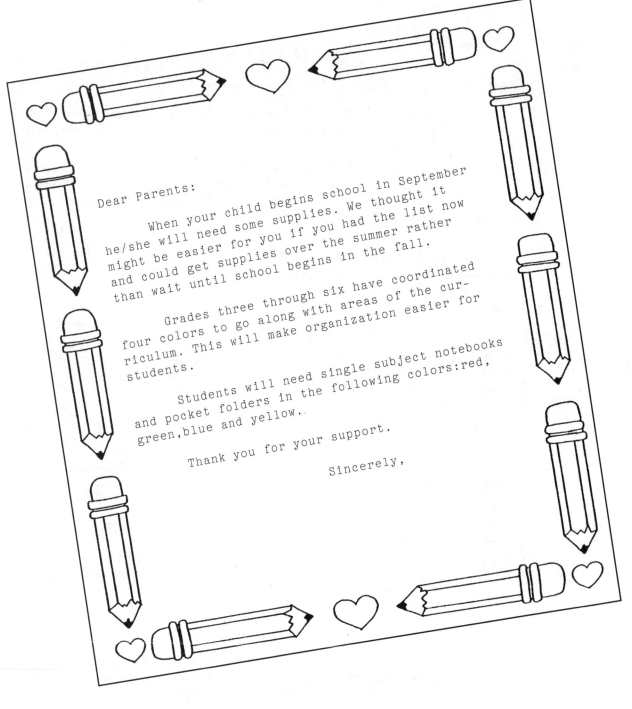

Dear Parents:

When your child begins school in September he/she will need some supplies. We thought it might be easier for you if you had the list now and could get supplies over the summer rather than wait until school begins in the fall.

Grades three through six have coordinated four colors to go along with areas of the curriculum. This will make organization easier for students.

Students will need single subject notebooks and pocket folders in the following colors:red, green,blue and yellow..

Thank you for your support.

Sincerely,

Work Folders (for younger students)

Each child uses a pocket folder to organize paperwork. The pocket folder has two pockets, one for finished work and one for unfinished work. All work must go into this folder.

Teachers need to be very explicit when work time is over. "If you are not done, take out your work folder and put your paper(s) in the unfinished pocket. Now look at your finished pocket. All papers you worked on and finished should be in that pocket."

Teachers may call out each assignment and have students hold their papers up, and then put them back in the appropriate pocket for practice. The two pockets may be labeled:

Unfinished	Finished
Not Completed	Completed
Need to work on	Done!

Teachers must continually remind students where the papers go.

Home/School Connection: Notices & Papers

Having a pocket folder specifically for take-home papers combined with an organizational time before and after school, helps students become more responsible for bringing the notices and papers back and forth from home to school.

Organizing Papers

Home/School Folder (for younger students)

The right hand pocket of the home/school folder is for important papers and notices that must go *right home*. Sometimes there are things that students need to keep at school that don't really fit into a subject folder. That's where the left side of this pocket folder comes in. Papers in the left hand side get *left at school*.

Home/School Envelope

My students use manila envelopes that travel home on a daily basis. Papers, notices, notes from me, menus, permission slips all go into the envelopes. The envelopes are kept in a box near the door. As students arrive in the morning they place their envelopes in the box. Before they leave at the end of each day, the envelopes are passed back. Parents know that the envelope will be taken home every day and should be brought back to school the following morning. All correspondence goes into the envelope. If a parent has something for me — a message, note, direction or question — it goes into the envelope.

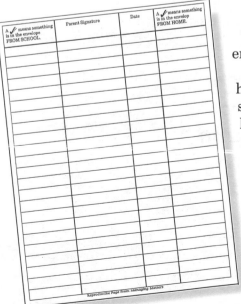

The form on page 25 is stapled on the front of each envelope.

This form has a place for a teacher to indicate if she has put anything in the envelope, a place for parents to sign-off daily, and a place for parents to indicate if they have sent anything back to school. This way teachers do not have to open and look in every envelope, only the ones that have a check from parents.

A ✔ means something is in the envelope FROM SCHOOL.	Parent Signature	Date	A ✔ means something is in the envelope FROM HOME.
A ✔ means something is in the envelope FROM SCHOOL.	Parent Signature	Date	A ✔ means something is in the envelope FROM HOME.

Reproducible

TOOT What Do I Do?

	M	T	W	Th	F
1. Desk Clean					
2. Classroom Job _____					
3. Get Lunchbox & Backpack					
4. Take Home Folder					
5. Put a SHARPENED pencil on your shelf					
6. Hat, Coat, Mittens Boots					

OT   What Do I Do?

	M	T	W	Th	F
1. **Desk/Locker Clean**	☐	☐	☐	☐	☐
2. **Assignment Notebook**	☐	☐	☐	☐	☐
Papers, Books					

<u>What resources do I need?</u>

	M	T	W	Th	F
Science	☐	☐	☐	☐	☐
Social Studies	☐	☐	☐	☐	☐
Math	☐	☐	☐	☐	☐
Language Arts					
Reading	☐	☐	☐	☐	☐
Writing	☐	☐	☐	☐	☐
Spelling	☐	☐	☐	☐	☐
3. Check Calendar Add to Assignment Book	☐	☐	☐	☐	☐
4. Take Home Folder Mailbox	☐	☐	☐	☐	☐

SAMPLE

DESK CLEAN

	M	T	W	Th	F
1. Take everything out	☐	☐	☐	☐	☐
2. Put back books	☐	☐	☐	☐	☐
3. Pile the loose papers	☐	☐	☐	☐	☐
4. Put loose papers in colored folders	☐	☐	☐	☐	☐
5. Put colored folders back in desk	☐	☐	☐	☐	☐
6. Put back pencils, markers, etc.	☐	☐	☐	☐	☐
7. Bring everything else up to your teacher	☐	☐	☐	☐	☐

Strategies to Help Students
Organize Information and Make Connections

The previous section offered many ideas and strategies to help students with physical organization — the *STUFF*. Some learners also have a difficult time organizing all the information they are learning, and this affects their achievement. This section gives strategies to help students organize information and make connections.

Eric Jensen, in his 1998 book titled *Introduction to Brain Compatible Learning,* states:

"The brain is meaning-driven. Meaning is more critical to the brain than information."

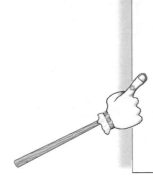

The classroom implication for Jensen's research is that we need to help students organize and learn in ways that make sense to them and are meaningful to their experiences.

We need to help students organize new information and concepts so that they link the new to the known. When students organize in this fashion everything is connected to something else. Research has shown that we learn best when we can connect a new experience to something that is familiar. Think about a time when you have had to explain something new to someone. Did you say...

"Remember when we did this...."
"It kind of looks like this...."
"It's similar to ...."

It is important to help students begin to organize and learn information in a way that makes sense to them and is meaningful to their experiences.

Using **Think Alouds** is an effective way to help students make learning more meaningful.

What Are Think Alouds?

Think Alouds are the verbalizations of what a student is thinking as he problem solves. Think Alouds help students monitor their learning and application of strategies. For struggling students Think Alouds often help show them that they are NOT using any strategies to help them with their learning. This awareness of their own thinking process is very powerful.

Think Alouds also help students understand concepts by helping them hook the unknown to the known. Think Alouds should be used on a daily basis in all areas of the curriculum.

Think Alouds can be used while students are:

- learning new concepts
- working with *old* concepts that are still difficult
- studying for tests

Why Use Think Alouds?

I. Think Alouds allow the struggling student to get into the minds of the proficient learner and ask:

"What are you doing?"
"Why do you understand this and I don't?"
"How are you remembering and understanding these concepts?"
"How are you organizing the information?"

II. Think Alouds help proficient learners become aware of their learning strategies.

III. Think Alouds let students see that one way is not the best.

IV. Think Alouds show students HOW to help each other.

Modeling Think Alouds

Teaching children to use Think Alouds requires endless modeling. Students need to see and hear Think Alouds modeled on a daily basis with school-related curriculum, as well as authentic examples of how we use them in our adult lives. For example, I told my students that after meeting my teacher's aide, who was named Cheryl Alander, I had a difficult time remembering her last name.

She helped by telling me to remember that she does the calendar each morning with our students, and her last name Alander rhymes with calendar. Modeling effective thinking skills helps students learn what to do when they get stuck.

Teacher to Student

Model Think Alouds during guided reading lessons. When a child gets stuck, Think Aloud the strategies you would use to help yourself through the problem: "Does this make sense? Does it sound right? Does it look right? I'm going to look at the pictures to see if they help me."

Student to Student

We teach concepts and information in the ways that we understand them. The way we understand things and our experiences can be so different from our students'. I think about the times that I have worked with a student (Jack) who is having difficulties understanding a concept. I have given Jack the information ten times and he still doesn't get it! But when I analyze the way I am giving the information it is no different each time. By the tenth time I am giving the SAME information LOUDER and SLOWER, but still the same way.

Then Janine, a student in the class who has no difficulty with learning, will say, "Hey Jack, think of it this way...." Carla, another peer, will add her understanding of the concept, and Pat will also give her suggestions to Jack. All of a sudden Jack *gets it*. Students need to hear information from each other. By hearing all of the different suggestions from Janine, Carla and Pat, Jack learns that one way is not best. Struggling learners need to hear how proficient learners are organizing and connecting new materials and information, and that they all do it a little differently.

Here is another example of how Think Alouds help students help each other. Judy was looking at a map of New York and was having difficulty remembering which city was to the east and which was to the west: Syracuse and Schenectady. Judy went to her friend Sara and asked her how she was remembering which city is where? Sara replied:

"We live in Connecticut. Syracuse is farther away from us than Schenectady, and Y is further down the alphabet than C. So Syracuse is farther west than Schenectady.

Think Aloud Cloud (for younger students)

Use the pattern on the next page to make a Think Aloud Cloud. Use oaktag and laminate it so it can last all year. Attach a headband to the cloud. Students pass around the Cloud and wear it as they Think Aloud and offer ways to remember and understand concepts.

Bounce an Idea (for older students)

Use a variety of different balls for students to throw to each other as they offer Think Alouds. Only one ball may be thrown at a time. Whoever has the ball does the Think Aloud. He then throws it to another child who catches it and does a Think Aloud. Some kinds of balls students have brought in are *Nerf* balls, footballs, *Koosh* balls, and rubber balls.

Our final goal should be for Think Aloud behavior to become eventually internalized. So it is our job to model and teach Think Aloud strategies in very explicit ways. Below are some ways to incorporate Think Aloud routines in your classroom.

Think Aloud Cloud

A Closer Look
A Real Life Classroom Example

Students are often given final assessments at the end of each year, especially older students, in the areas of science and social studies. They are basically asked what they remember about units that were studied months ago. It is always so frustrating when they remember NOTHING, or very little. I've often wondered how they can spend the whole year with me and not remember anything that we learned. I now understand that this was their way of saying to me they were learning information for the week only, not as life-long learners.

The ocean Think Aloud below was done with my class in October. Students were responsible for knowing the following information:

· The three levels of ocean life: Plankton, Nekton, Benthos

· Examples and characteristics of animals at each level

The following pictures show examples of their Think Alouds. I drew the pictures and wrote notes on the board as students gave their ideas and suggestions.

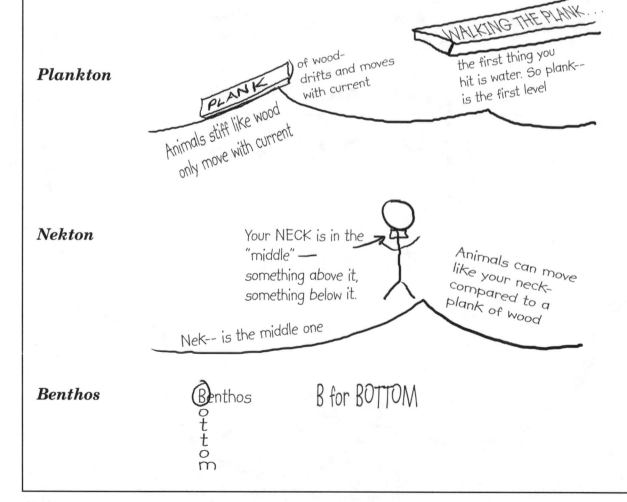

Plankton

Nekton

Benthos

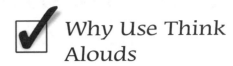

At the end of the school year students were asked to get a piece of paper and write down everything they remembered learning about the ocean unit. One struggling learner, Dom, (working significantly below grade level), yelled, "I don't remember nothing." He was just ready to become a behavior problem. Most of the time when this child thinks he is in over his head he shuts down and will not even try. If he doesn't try then he doesn't fail.

Dom was at a dead end. The Think Alouds gave him the turns or detours that he needed to make to get to the final destination: What have you learned about the ocean?

Just after he yelled this, one of his peers (John) said, "Hey Dom, remember this?" John was was pointing to and holding his own neck. Dom smiled and said, "Yeah the middle one is neck something." Another child (Vinnie) jumped in and told Dom to look at him. Vinnie was making his fingers walk. Dom again said, "Oh yeah, the top one is walking the plank . . . . Plank something." He went back to his seat and began writing. He understood and remembered plankton, nekton, and "Ben something." He could give examples of animals at each layer and what they did.

Think Alouds show students HOW to help each other. Notice how John and Vinnie helped Dom. They did not just give him the answer. They helped him by giving a clue or hint. When students are asked to help each other they oftentimes will just copy each other or give each other the answer. Now, after working with Think Alouds on a daily basis, students start giving each other help by making connections.

Student Interest and Motivation

The second foundational issue that teachers need to be aware of is students' interests and motivation, and how to use this information to help the classroom become a team. The more excitement and positive attitudes students bring to the learning environment, the easier and greater the achievement. If students are team players, everyone shares the good and bad times together. They learn how and when to support each other. Also, knowing your students' interests and attitudes can inform your teaching choices.

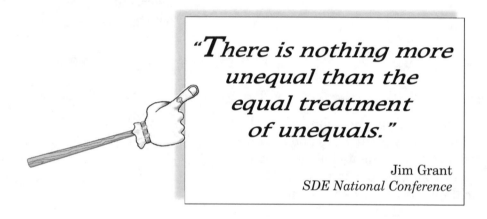

"*There is nothing more unequal than the equal treatment of unequals.*"

Jim Grant
SDE National Conference

The following activities help students understand that one way is not best. They help students to feel confident about their own work.

One Way is Not the Best (for older students)

Ask students to get a piece of paper and number it one through four. Give no other directions. Students might ask questions about what kind of paper to use or if they should skip lines between each number, but give them no suggestions. Also, ask students not to look at each other's papers. When they have completed the assignment ask the following questions.

How many students:

skipped one line between numbers?

skipped more than one line between numbers?

skipped no lines between numbers?

used lined paper?

put a circle around each number?

put a period next to each number?

put a parenthesis or half a circle around each number?

left each number alone?

You can record their answers on the board or chart paper.

This is one assignment, but look at all the different responses. Which one is the best? Which ones are correct? They all are! Students see that even though they might have written something different from their neighbor, they were all correct. Have students do some Think Alouds after this activity (see pages 30-35). They can share why they wrote the numbers the way they did and what they were thinking when the directions were given.

"It's Not Fair!" (for younger students)

The following activity, done early in the year, helps students understand and work with fairness issues. It shows how being part of a team benefits everyone.

All students need a pair of shoes that tie. If students do not have a pair that tie, then give them a pair to use. (I bring in tie shoes that I have at home and also ask my colleagues at school to bring some in to help me out. It doesn't matter what size the shoes are as long as they tie.) Have all of the students that are wearing tie shoes take them off. Students who are not wearing tie shoes do not need to take their shoes off. They will be using the pairs you supply.

Tell the students who took their shoes off to put them back on and tie them; and students who did not take their shoes off to tie the pair they were given. Tell students that as soon as they are finished tying, they should line up at the door and you will go out to recess, BUT no one can help anyone. I remind students that I can not help them because it wouldn't be fair if I helped one and not another. Some children can tie and line up right away. They have to wait until everyone is ready. They often immediately ask if they can help and I tell them "No, because it wouldn't be fair."

You will have to use your judgment as to when to stop this activity. I stop it when I see students who cannot tie beginning to get concerned.

When you stop this activity have students all sit together and talk about what happened. We discuss that we all have strengths and weaknesses. Make a banner that says: ***Fair is whatever you need to be successful!*** Some students may need help in math, some in reading, some with tying their shoes. Everyone also doesn't finish at the same time.

Now do this activity again, but as soon as students are done tying they can help someone else. The teacher can also help. Tell students as soon as all shoes are tied they can go out to recess. It is amazing how quickly they work together. Any time a child says, "that's not fair," remind him about this activity.

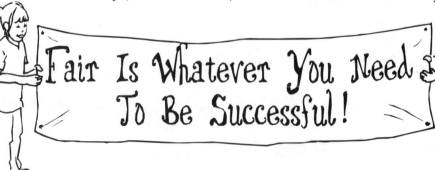

Fair Is Whatever You Need To Be Successful!

It Takes Two

Pair students together. Give them an assignment or an activity to do such as:

- make a peanut butter and jelly sandwich
- make a tower with Unifix cubes
- create a design with a geoboard
- fold a piece of paper in half, thirds, quarters
- trace a stencil

Sounds easy enough, but each student can only use one hand. They must put one of their arms behind their back and keep it there throughout the activity.

Students must depend on each other to complete the assignment. They need to be able to communicate their desires and suggestions to each other and work together. Make sure students realize this is not a race and there is no winner. To prevent competition have another activity ready for partners to complete so no one finishes "last."

Decision Making and Ownership

Students need to feel part of a team in the classroom. All students should be responsible for sharing, taking turns, making decisions, completing chores or doing special activities. Choosing children for all of these activities can be extremely difficult for the teacher. We need to make sure everyone gets a turn and that everyone is a part of the decisions that are made on a daily basis. Sometimes the passive learner, or struggling learner, is not an integral part of all these activities because he is not vocal or other students just take over. In and Out Cans can be used to ensure that everyone has a part in decision making, and therefore ownership is strong.

In & Out Cans

How to Make In and Out Cans

There are two cans in the classroom, an IN can and an OUT can. All of the students' names are put in the IN can. Any time a decision needs to be made, pull a name from the IN can. That is the child who makes the decision. His name then goes in the OUT can. Everyone is a winner because everyone gets to make a decision at some point.

You can also use clothespins instead of pieces of paper. Write each child's name on a clothespin and snap it onto the IN can. As each student gets a turn, their name gets unclipped from the IN can and gets clipped onto the OUT can.

Picking Volunteers

The cans can be used for just about everything that comes up during the day. For example, if someone comes into the classroom and asks for three volunteers, just pull three names from the IN can. You don't have to pick three children. No matter how hard we try, someone always says, "You never pick me." That doesn't happen anymore.

Everyone Has a Chance

The cans can be used during whole group discussions and mini-lessons. During whole group instruction, some students are waving their hands and making noise, before we even finish asking the question. Students who need more think time are then thrown off and lose interest because their peers already know the answer. Passive learners then tend never to raise their hands. They just sit back and let others answer questions.

Keeping Students Attentive

During small group or whole group activities, no one may raise their hand. After a question is asked, pick a name from one of the cans. This makes all students participate and keeps them attentive because they never know whose name is going to be picked. This is the only time that the teacher can pick names from either can, and after names are picked they go back into the same can. The name may be pulled out again. Otherwise after the child's name is picked, he thinks he can "tune out" because his name has already been chosen and will not be pulled again.

Active Learners

What happens if the child whose name gets picked does not know the answer? Can students pass if they don't want to answer or do the activity? Many teachers commented that they let students pass if they wished, but then the same children always said "pass," or five children would pass in a row and then it became the "thing to do." Our original problem now is present again. Students can become passive because they know they can pass. Students can tune out and not be risk takers because they can pass.

I work the cans so that nobody is allowed to pass. If a child does not know the answer or is having a difficult time responding, then the following options can be explored:

- rephrase the question
- ask for only a piece of the answer
- ask another question that is related to what is being asked
- give the child a hint or prompt

Inventories

Inventories are great ways to find out and access information about your students. Inventories can help teachers gain awareness into many areas of a child's life such as:

- likes and dislikes
- home
- friends
- strengths and weaknesses
- work preferences
- how the child processes information

The list is endless!

Reading Inventory

This inventory is completed by students in September and then again at the end of the school year. The goal is to see an increased awareness of strategies and a love of reading and writing by the end of the year, as reflected in the second inventory. Students who are able fill out the inventories themselves do. If reading and writing are difficult, then students can dictate to the teacher and she fills out their inventories.

Use responses #1,#2, and #5 to inform you about each student's attitude toward reading.

Use responses #3 and #4 to learn about each student's reading preferences.

Reading Inventory

Name   Date

1. How do you feel about reading?

2. Do you think you are a good reader? Why?

3. What was the last book you read?

4. What kinds of books do you like to read?

5. Do you think it is important to be a good reader?

   Why?

Use response #6 to learn what strategies each student uses for decoding.

Use responses #7 and #8 to learn about each student's reading habits.

Use response #9 to inform you about each student's attitude toward reading.

Use response #10 to learn about your students' preferences.

6. What do you do when you come to a word you can't read?

7. Do you read at home?

8. What do you usually do after school when you get home?

9. Do you like to read? Why?

10. Is there anything you would like me to know that would help you have a good year at school?

This inventory is one that has been used to gain information about children's reading habits, preferences, attitude/feelings and strategies.

Reading Inventory

Name _____ Date _____

1. How do you feel about reading?

2. Do you think you are a good reader? Why?

3. What was the last book you read?

4. What kinds of books do you like to read?

5. Do you think it is important to be a good reader? Why?

6. What do you do when you come to a word you can't read?

7. Do you read at home?

8. What do you usually do after school when you get home?

9. Do you like to read? Why?

10. Is there anything you would like me to know that would help you
    have a good year at school?

A Closer Look
A Real Life Classroom Example

 I used the September Inventory to inform my approach to teaching Tom reading.

Here is a Reading Inventory filled out by Tom, a fourth grader, who is a struggling learner. On the left are his September responses, and on the right, his June responses.

#5 I learned that Tom did not see a need for reading. I also learned what his interests were by using the Interest Interview on page 49.

One of my teaching goals was to show Tom why he needs to be able to read, using reasons he'd be interested in. For example:

- directions for putting his models together
- instructions for new games that were brought into the classroom
- rules for baseball when a question came up
- lunch menus for the week
- TV guide, etc.

#4 Tom likes mysteries, so most of the books I used for his reading instruction in September were mysteries.

Reading Inventory

Name _Tom_   Date _September 9_

1. How do you feel about reading?

   I like reading.

2. Do you think you are a good reader? Why?

   no becus it is hard !

3. What was the last book you read?

   Freckil Jusie

4. What kinds of books do you like to read?

   mistreys

5. Do you think it is important to be a good reader? Why?

   no they are poring.

6. What do you do when you come to a word you can't read?

   Sond it out

7. Do you read at home?

   Sometimes

8. What do you usually do after school when you get home?

   go play soker

9. Do you like to read? Why?

   yes becus yu can learn

10. Is there any thing you would like me to know that would help you have a good year at school?

    I don't like working in Big grops

Reading Inventory

Name _Tom_   Date _June 4_

1. How do you feel about reading?

   Very good

2. Do you think you are a good reader? Why?

   yes because at the beging of The year I didnt like reading

3. What was the last book you read?

   The Coller Citlings

4. What kinds of books do you like to read?

   yes because you can read instruckings

5. Do you think it is important to be a good reader? Why?

   funneye

I used the June inventory to assess Tom's growth as a reader.

#2 Notice in September he has no confidence in himself as a reader. Look at the change at the end of the year.

#5 In September he sees no reason to be a reader. There is an incredible shift in June when he sees the need to read. (We have been working on reading directions to put together models and to learn rules to some games he has brought in.)

#6 He goes from one strategy (sound it out) to two strategies (skip it and read on and find the spelling pattern.)

#7 His response changes from sometimes to YES!

#8 By the end of the year he is reading at home, not just in school.

#9 His first answer is a great "teacher" answer. The ownership is on us. But in his June response he shifts the ownership to himself. HE likes to read.

#10 He has gone from a negative statement to a positive. He is feeling more confident about working in groups.

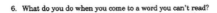

6. What do you do when you come to a word you can't read?

   SKip it and read on find the Spelling pardin

7. Do you read at home?

   yes

8. What do you usually do after school when you get home?

   ridemy bike   read

9. Do you like to read? Why?

   yes because reading is fun

10. Is there any thing you would like me to know that would help you have a good year at school?

    I like small grops

Interviews

Interviews are a great way to gather information about your students. You may have a number of set questions you want to ask, or you might ask the class to talk about what questions they feel would be important to ask. Interviews can last from 5-15 minutes. If you interview two-three students each day at the beginning of the year, within the first three weeks you will have interviewed everyone.

Interest Interview

The interest interview found on the next page is one that has been used to gain information about children's interests, likes and dislikes. This interview is completed once a year in September. Use students' answers to ensure that books and items of interest are available in the classroom. Refer to their interests and strengths as often as possible. This interview could also be set up as an inventory where students write out their answers.

Interest Interview

Name _Tom_   Date _September 21_

1. What is your favorite thing to do at home?   at school?

    Play baseball   lunch and games

2. What is your least favorite thing to do at home?   at school?

    cleaning my room   reading

3. Do you collect anything?

    models

4. What can you do well?

    Sports, models

5. What is difficult for you to do?

    Working in big grops

6. Do you watch television? What are your favorite shows?

    yes!   I love all cartoons

7. What are you interested in?

    Putting together model plans and ships

Interest Interview

Name _____   Date _____

1. What is your favorite thing to do at home?   at school?

2. What is your least favorite thing to do at home?   at school?

3. Do you collect anything?

4. What can you do well?

5. What is difficult for you to do?

6. Do you watch television? What are your favorite shows?

7. What are you interested in?

"The best teacher is not necessarily
the one who possesses the most
knowledge, but the one who
most effectively enables
his students to believe in their
ability to learn."

Norma Cousins

From: *The Heart and Wisdom of Teaching*
Compiled by Esther Wright

Part 2
Strategies & Activities
for Language Arts

Three Cueing Systems

There are three cueing systems that readers need to access. Proficient readers utilize all three language cueing systems listed below.

- **Syntactic or Language System**
  This refers to the structure of our language; can you say it that way in English? Is it grammatically correct?

- **Semantics System**
  This refers to meaning; does it make sense?

- **Visual or Graphophonics System**
  This refers to phonics, letters, and sounds.

If students overuse or ignore a system, reading difficulties can occur.

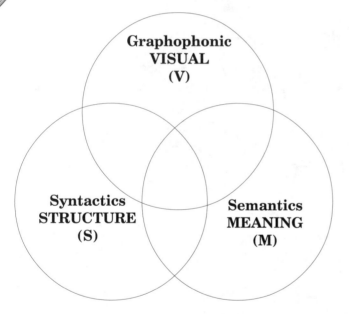

If a child uses the graphophonic (V) system to the extreme, he may become a word caller. This is a child who sees a letter P and gives you everything he can think of that starts with a P with no regard to semantics (M) or syntactics (S). This is a child who will often just guess at words.

If a child uses the (S) and (M) systems to the extreme, he may become a child who can tell a beautiful story that makes sense but has nothing to do with the print on the page. This may be a child who tries to read by the pictures rather than the print and the pictures.

Our goal is to help students become proficient readers by using all three systems.

Prompting Language

There are certain prompting questions that can help students begin to use all three systems when they are reading or when they get stuck. Two exceptional resources for building a repertoire of strategic, successful prompts are the books *Guided Reading* by Irene Fountas and Gay Su Pinnell, page 161, and *Invitations* by Regie Routman, page 140.

A Closer Look
A Real Life Classroom Example

Pay attention to your prompting language. If it is consistent, then students will apply it and use it when reading alone because they can "hear you" in their minds. Also, be aware of the strategies you use to help students. For example, a sentence might read:

Kristi and Raymond fed their parakeet.

If the child is having difficulty with the word *parakeet*, be aware of giving the clue:

It is a kind of bird.

That kind of prompt will not help students when they are reading independently. You have not given the student a strategy to use; instead you have created a guessing game. It will work, but only in that isolated example. Instead use consistent prompts that can help them attack any word, not just the word parakeet. For example, when working with Stacie, a second grader, the following conversation took place:

Teacher	"What would make sense in that sentence?"
Stacie	"Some kind of animal. I think it's a dog."
Teacher	"You're right, DOG would make sense, and it sounds right. But does it look right?"
Stacie	"Oh no, dog has a D. The animal has to start with a P."
Teacher	"Is there a part of the word that you know?"
Stacie	"I see *keet* at the end... P...keet...Parakeet! Kristi and Raymond fed their parakeet."

Strategy Poster

Make a poster with one key question from each cueing system. I have chosen: Does it look right? Does it sound right? Does it make sense? Display the poster prominently in your classroom so students can refer to it when they get stuck. Put a visual next to each question to help students who may have difficulty reading the poster. Your poster may look something like this:

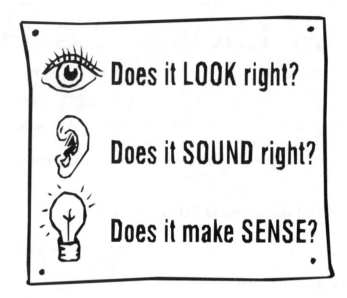

Strategy Cards

Give each child an index card with the three prompting questions on it, one from each system. Have each student draw a picture next to the questions. Laminate the cards. Students should always have these index cards with them when they are reading independently. These cards can be their bookmarks. Before silent reading each day I always remind students to bring their *strategies* with them.

Cloze Activities

Cloze activities are an effective way to help students apply and utilize the three cueing systems when reading. Cloze activities can be used in a variety of ways.

Cloze Activities

Individual Sentences

Write a series of sentences on the board with one word missing. For example:

> We are having _____ for dinner.
> We are having h ____ for dinner.
> We are having hotd ____ for dinner.

We are having _____

pizza
hambugers
chicken
hotdogs
macaroni

Show students only the first sentence and have them brainstorm what words would make sense in the blank. Write down all of their responses. This step uses the M and S systems.

We are having h_____

~~pizza~~
hambugers
~~chicken~~
hotdogs
~~macaroni~~

Now show students the second sentence and have them decide which of their predictions could be correct based on the new visual information. This step uses the M, S and V systems.

~~pizza~~
hambugers
~~chicken~~
hotdogs
~~macaroni~~

We are having hotd _____

Show students the third sentence and have them make their final prediction. This step also uses the M, S and V systems, with more emphasis now on V.

This activity helps the struggling reader who is a word caller. (He looks at the first letter and calls any word he can think of that begins with that letter with no regard to meaning.) The child now has to key in on meaning first.

Strategies & Activities for Language Arts

Big Books and Post-It® Notes

A similar activity can be used with big books and *Post-It* notes. Take a *Post-It* and cover up a word in the sentence. Have students predict what the word might be using the cueing systems of sense and meaning. Then fold over the *Post-It* to reveal the first letter and have them look at their predictions and make some more decisions now based on the visual cueing system.

Morning Messages

Morning messages are another resource to use with the cloze procedure. Below is a morning message with *Post-It* notes.

Decoding and Spelling with Pattern Words

Two types of words will be explored in this section. First, we will look at words that follow rules and patterns. These activities and ideas will tie into your phonics program, reading instruction and parts of your spelling program. Then we will look at sight words and the most commonly misspelled words. These words do not fit into your phonics program because most have no rules or patterns. They will tie into your reading program and part of your spelling program.

Pattern Word Wall

Decoding and spelling of pattern words go hand in hand. One of the biggest problems students have is remembering and using all of those patterns and rules that are taught.

Word Wall

Set up a "wall" in the classroom where there is a representation of everything that has been taught in the spelling/decoding area. This does a number of things:

- ✔ When students say they don't remember, it refers them to a place that has an example of a familiar, already studied concept.

- ✔ There is a representation of everything that has been taught.

- ✔ Students don't need to memorize, they can utilize and apply.

- ✔ It offers a direction when students are at a dead end. (See page 132)

- ✔ If a student does not understand a concept when it is first taught, it allows him to see it every day for the rest of the year so he can make the connection whenever he is ready.

- ✔ It keeps skills current.

Decoding and spelling walls can be used throughout the grades. The strategies are the same, what is different are the rules, patterns, combinations, etc., that are appropriate for each grade level. These "walls" need to be built and created WITH YOUR STUDENTS!

Strategies & Activities for Language Arts

Involve Your Students

Strategies are not very effective and efficient when students have no part in setting them up. Decoding and spelling walls start BLANK at the beginning of the year. Nothing is there. They get created with students as they learn different concepts in our curriculums.

Organizing the Wall

The wall gets created as you teach each new rule or pattern. It needs to be set up and organized according to your curriculum. My wall was organized by vowels because that seemed to be the hardest part for students. They did okay with beginning and ending sounds, but the middle stuff was difficult for them. Also, that is how my curriculum was organized.

Putting Words on the Wall

Each week as you introduce a new concept, pattern or rule, brainstorm all of the words that fit that specific rule. Then pick one word to represent each pattern/rule taught and place it on the word wall (see page 59 for how to choose words). Usually you will add one to two words a week depending on your curriculum.

Patricia Cunningham and Dorothy Hall have three excellent references for lists of word patterns: *Making Words, Making More Words*, and *Making Big Words. Phonics Patterns* by Edward Fry is another good resource.

a	e	i	o	u		Other				
cat	pet	fit	rob	cut	moon	look	cow	toy	all
	bread				grew		mouse	oil	haul
					through				caught
make	feel	time	nose	cube					
tail	deal	pie	coat				question		
pay	happy	my	crow				mission		
eight	chief	night							
	either								

Above is an example of a word wall that I used with my students. Please keep in mind that this was created and organized around my specific curriculum with my students. Your wall may look and be organized in a completely different way. The key is to have one representation of everything you have taught all year for students to be able to refer to. Putting up pictures along with the words helps learners who need just a little more support. Remember, this is a wall for pattern words only. Sight words (see pages 67-74) go in a separate space.

Choosing Words

We used to use majority vote to decide on the words that would represent each pattern or rule, but there are many problems with this:

- It takes too long.

- There is always a loser.

- Winners oftentimes brag that their choice won.

- If a student's word/vote has not been chosen for three weeks in a row, that child often has no motivation to use the wall as a strategy.

We rarely, if ever, use majority vote any more. Whenever a decision needs to be made I pull a name from the IN can. That determines who makes the decision. Everyone gets a turn to choose a word. Everyone owns and has input into the wall. See pages 40-41 for more information about using these cans.

Teaching Students to Use the Wall

Reference the word wall all the time for spelling and decoding. When a child asks how to spell a word, he can be guided to look at the word wall. For example, if a child spelled the word RIGHT, R-I-T, he would be asked to look at the word NIGHT to help him spell RIGHT. The biggest change I saw in my students was the way they asked for help. They weren't coming up to me just asking me how to spell a word, but were instead saying, "I'm trying to spell the word boat. Is it like coat or like nose?"

In addition to posting these word lists, students need lots of experiences with them. Regie Routman writes:

"... A skill—no matter how well it has been taught cannot be considered a strategy until the learner can use it purposefully and independently....The learner must know how and when to apply the skill; that is what elevates it to the strategy level."

Regie Routman
Transitions

A skill stays a skill as long as it is memorized and learned only for a week. It doesn't become a strategy until it is utilized and applied. The next several pages offer ideas for practical daily use.

Turning Skills Into Strategies

The Have-A-Go sheet found on page 63 has been adapted from Regie Routman's original found in her book *Invitations*.

Use the Have-A-Go sheets every day for five minutes with your whole class. Also use Have-A-Go three to five times a week with your strugglers in a small group setting. Students need to make the connection that the word wall will help them read, decode, spell and write words when they are stuck, as they often do not make the connection between spelling, reading, and writing.

Have-A-Go

How to Use Have-A-Go sheets

Each child has a Have-A-Go sheet in front of him. The sheets can be used many different ways. One way is to ask students to "Have a go writing the word TRAY," for example. Students try to write it on the left side of their paper under First Attempt. After they have tried once, brainstorm as a class or group. Talk about patterns and sounds. Brainstorm the different options you might have to write the word.

The last thing to say to students is, "Look at the word wall. If you know the word PAY, then you know the word TRAY. PAY helps you read, decode, spell, and write the word TRAY. Now try to write the word TRAY again." (The word PAY is on the word wall because the long /a/ sound, spelled /ay/, has already been taught, and the word pay was chosen to represent that pattern.)

Students then try to write the word in the middle column titled Try Again/Edit. After they have tried again, model how to use the word **pay** to help with the word **tray**. Write the word TRAY on the board.

Students then write the word in the right column of their paper titled Standard Spelling.

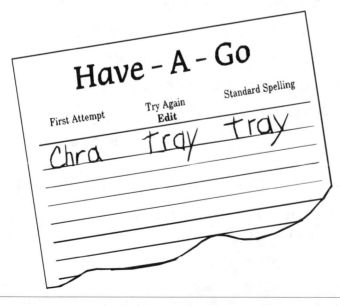

Review Skills

When using Have-A-Go, try to work with patterns and sounds that have already been taught. Many times students are doing fine with this week's lessons. It is last week's curriculum and the one from five months ago that they forgot and don't use. This activity helps keep skills current for students. Ask students to make words plural, or add an *ing* ending or an *ed* ending, etc. Those are rules that students often memorize and then don't apply to their daily writing, especially if they have worked with them weeks or months ago.

Guided Reading

Another way to use the word wall and Have-A-Go sheets is while working with students in a guided reading lesson. You can usually use just one sheet for the group. When they read and get stuck on a word, ask them to look at the word wall and find a word that looks like the one they are stuck on. Ask, "Do you see/know any word like this word?" Write that word on the sheet and then use an analogy: If you know this, then you know this.

Writing Time

Students use the Have-A-Go sheets any time they are writing. Some younger students will write NOTHING unless it is spelled correctly. They have a difficult time taking risks and just writing what they hear. These sheets have been very successful in helping students become more independent writers. Students are not allowed to come up to the teacher and ask, "How do you spell this?" They have to have a sheet in their hand and have already tried the word. The first thing this does is force them to try and write something down. When they come up for help, you might check off the beginning sound and tell them they have the first sound and that's all they need. They will often ask if the rest is *right*. You might tell them whether it is or isn't correct, but reiterate that all they need right now is the first sound. This very quickly weans them away from coming up to you all the time.

Editing

The Have-A-Go sheets can also be used for editing. Students write down words from their writing that they are not sure are spelled correctly. Then they use both of the walls to help them edit.

Assessment

As students fill their Have-A-Go sheets they put them in their portfolios. Some students fill one sheet a week, while others fill six or seven. At the end of each month, go through each child's Have-A-Go sheets and keep two, a high and a low. Keep one that shows an excellent use of the word wall and analogies. Keep another that shows something the child couldn't do but should have been able to. All the rest get stapled and go home. These are fantastic anecdotal records. They let you glimpse into the minds of your students to see how they are processing this information, what they hear and how they put things together.

Inform Your Teaching

Another added bonus you'll find when looking through Have-A-Go sheets is seeing class trends. For example, when I asked my first graders to try to write the word tray, more than half of the class wrote *chra*. When fourth graders were asked to make *jump, jumped*, more than half of them put a T at the end.

Have – A – Go

First Attempt	Try Again **Edit**	Standard Spelling

Adapted from Routman's **Have-A-Go**, *Invitations*, Heinemann, 1991.

Reproducible

More Ways to Practice and Use Spelling Patterns and Rules

We must provide students with many opportunities to use, practice, and play with words. Below are some suggestions.

Practice with Pattern Words

Plastic Letters

Assemble a baggie of letters that coordinates with each rule and pattern that you teach. Students benefit by touching, moving, and manipulating words. In the baggie are red letters that represent the pattern being taught, the *rimes*. There are also blue letters that can be used to make words using the patterns, the *onsets*. Students take out the letters from the baggie and make as many words as they can. Also put in onsets that do not make words when added to the rimes. My students then have to make a list of real words and nonsense words.

Rhyming Riddles

Read the book *One Sun, A Book of Terse Verse* by Bruce McMillan. Each page in this book has a picture of something that is described in two words. For example, there is a picture of a hand that is full of sand, a sand-hand. There is a picture of a stone all by itself, a lone-stone. Have students come up with riddles as you read each page. The riddles have been referred to as Hink Pinks. For example:

What would you call your hand after you've been at the beach making sand castles all day?
a sand-hand

What would you call a rock that was all by itself?
a lone-stone

What would you call a gentleman who has been in the sun all day?
a tan-man

After modeling with this book, have students make up their own riddles with the specific patterns and rules you are teaching. The first step is to generate a list of words with the whole class. For example, if you were working with the A-Consonant-E pattern your list might include: bake, cake, rake, take, lake, fake, flake, make, grate, gate, Kate. Write these words on a piece of chart paper that can be displayed and added to all week. During independent work time students can refer to this chart to make their own riddles. Some riddles students came up with for these words are:

What would you call something that is chocolate and you eat with icing that is in the shape of a garden tool?
a rake-cake

What would you call an entrance in a fence that you couldn't use?
a fake-gate

You can be as general or specific about the pattern as you choose. Notice in the example above that AKE and ATE patterns were both used for A-Consonant-E. You can be more specific and just use AKE words or ATE words.

Highlighting Tape

After reading a book, students can use highlighting tape (see page 103) to highlight words containing the pattern and rules being taught.

Flipbooks

If students are working with rules they can make a flipbook (see pages 91-102) to categorize the words according to the rule. For example, if working with plurals, the outside flaps might be labeled:

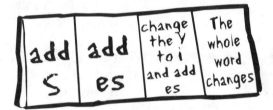

Students would write each word under the correct flap according to the rule.

You could do the same thing for adding ING and ED endings. The outside flaps might be labeled:

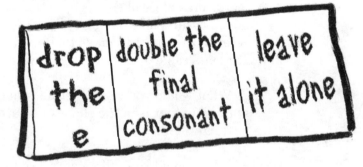

If working with the long /a/ sound, the outside flaps might be labeled:

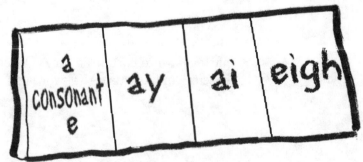

Decoding and Spelling with Sight Words

Pattern words and words that follow rules help students with decoding, phonics, and spelling. But what about the words that do not fit patterns, such as sight words and most commonly misspelled words? Using the pattern word wall to try and figure these out will not help students. It may even confuse them because they will be using an inappropriate strategy.

Sight Words

A Separate Place

Next to your pattern word wall have another section that deals with these tricky words. This wall also starts BLANK at the beginning of each year. It is built and created with students. Students have named this place in the classroom many different things:

Just Gotta Know 'Em Words

Outlaw Words

Jail Words

Weird Words

Renegades

Rule Busters

This wall is set up in alphabetical order. As students learn and come across these words in their reading and writing, we write them together on a piece of paper and hang them up as a class or group of students.

Create Visuals

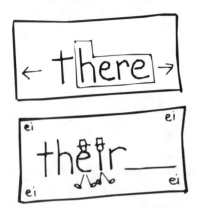

Placing a visual next to each word often helps students *see* the word. Below are some examples that came from students.

We were working with the words THERE and THEIR. With the word THERE, they said to configure the word *here* and put in arrows because this word usually means a place. Is it over here or there?

For the word THEIR, students said to turn the vowels into people and put a line right after the word because with this word it is usually two people or things that own something. And what they own is usually right after the word. For example:

> It is their homework.
> It is their dog.

Have-A-Go

When using the Have-A-Go sheets, explained on pages 60-63, also have students write these tricky words. Ask them to try and not look at the wall but visualize the word and its picture. If they look at the word that is fine because it gets them to realize that the wall really does work as a strategy.

Look Cover Write Check

Introduce this strategy in a whole group or small group setting. Students need to see this modeled a number of times before it becomes an effective and efficient strategy.

This strategy helps students:

- study for spelling tests
- analyze words they are having difficulty with
- practice the most commonly misspelled words

Sight Words

How to Use Look Cover Write Check

STEP 1:   Use the sheet found on page 72. Have students fold it in half, and then in half again.

STEP 2:   Students begin in the column labeled Look 1. They write down any word(s) they are having difficulty with. They can work with one word or their entire list of spelling words. Next to each word have them make a square or a circle. This acts as a place keeper so they don't skip any words.

STEP 3:   After students have written down all the words they will be working with, they should look back at the first word they wrote. Tell students to:

- **Look** at the whole word.

- **Underline** the word as you say it.

- **Configure** the word.

- **Cover** the word with the Cover 2 flap.

- **Write** the word without looking at it.

While students are writing, tell them to visualize the word and picture the configuration. After writing the word, they check it by taking back the Cover 2 flap. If the word is misspelled, they should not erase. They need to analyze and study their mistake and then rewrite the word correctly under the misspelled word.

Finally, students must think of how to remember where the problem is in the word and how to remember the correct spelling. Then they repeat the process in the last column.

A Closer Look
A Real Life Classroom Example

Look Cover Write Check

Michael, a third grader, was working with the word TABLE. He wrote t-a-b-e-l in his third column.

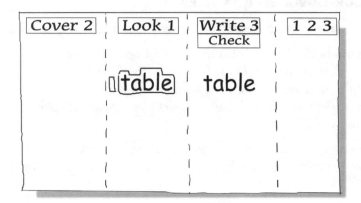

When he unfolded his flap he saw his mistake. His clue to remember the ending of the word was: "... **e-l** at the end of a word is like a step up. **L-e** at the end of a word is like a step down. Table has a step down at the end. If I were standing on the table, mom would tell me to step down. So I can remember the end, where my mistake is, because I'll picture myself stepping down off the table."

 Assign the Look, Cover, Write, Check as homework Thursday night as a way for students to study for a spelling test.

A Closer Look
A Real Life Classroom Example

My students love to use the word *scary* in their writing. This word was one that I constantly had to look up in the dictionary. I would forget if it was spelled *scarey* or *scary*.

Scarey or Scary?

One day Alisha came up to me and asked how to spell scary. I told her to get me the dictionary. She looked at me and said, exasperated, "You looked it up yesterday!" I told Alisha it was one of my tough words.

She suggested that I do a Look, Cover, Write, Check and ask the class for suggestions.

So that's just what we did. I put the sheet on the overhead and worked through it as my students watched. We realized it was the ending that was tricky. We brainstormed some ways I could remember there is no *e* at the end.

Clara said, "If you are really scared, you want to get out of there FAST. You don't have time to write the *e*." Barry added "Get in your car and go." I don't think twice now about the spelling of scary. It has no *e*. Working through and modeling problems we have as adults with learning is a powerful tool for students. This is also an example of modeling with Think Alouds (see pages 30-35).

1 2 3

Write 3
Check

Look 1

Cover 2

Glue Words

Cut oaktag into 4x6 inch pieces. Mix tempera paint into white glue and write the sight words that students are having difficulty with on each card with the glue. Let the cards sit over night to dry. Students do four things with these glue words. They:

Rub It

Put a piece of paper over the glue words and do a rubbing with a crayon.

Trace It

Take the piece of paper off the glue word and trace it.

Write It

Write the word under the traced rubbing.

Use It

This part of the glue word activity can be stretched up or down depending on your student's abilities. Tell your students to:

- Use the word in a sentence.
- Draw a picture of it.
- Give some synonyms.
- Give some antonyms.

A Closer Look
A Real Life Classroom Example

The following are three samples of **Use It** from the same first grade classroom working with **Glue Words**.

Cathi is a struggling learner. She will write nothing if she doesn't know how to spell it. She is very comfortable with pictures. Cathi knows she can *write* anything in picture form. We know she understands the word *said* by her picture.

Eric is at grade level, maybe a little above, maybe a little below. He is right there in the middle.

Connie is working well above grade level. She has no difficulties with reading and writing. She doesn't need work on recognizing and spelling the word *said*, so she does a lot with vocabulary development. She wrote about 20 words instead of *said* for her Use It.

Connie

Stated
Thought
Whimpered
panted
Shouted
hollered
answered
Spoke
Voiced
uttered
screamed
repeated
demanded
proclaimed
announced

Pulling It All Together

Students who are pulled out for extra help, or work with more than one teacher in more than one classroom often say, "Where is the word wall? I need it." Traveling strategy folders is a solution to this problem.

Traveling Strategy Folders

Traveling strategy folders help students refer to the word walls and other reading strategies when they are reading and writing independently.

Traveling strategy folders are easily made with file folders. There are four sides to the folders. Choose four key strategies that you feel your students need right next to them every time they are reading and writing. I always include the pattern word wall and Just Gotta Know 'Em Words.

Managing traveling strategy folders (a monthly process)

Week 1

Students get copies of their classroom word walls on sheets of paper. Their papers match the classroom word walls exactly. For the pattern word wall, students need to highlight all of the patterns that are on their paper. This helps them review everything they have already learned. You can help by having the patterns already underlined.

For the Just Gotta Know 'Em (sight words) wall they could draw in the visuals for one to three words of their choice.

Weeks 2-4 Each week as the class adds to the word wall in the classroom, students add to their individual folders, usually one to two words per week. By the end of the fourth week, it will be hard to read some of your student's folders. The words won't line up, perhaps they wrote too big, etc. So the first week of each month the papers get ripped out and thrown away and a new one gets taped or stapled in. The new traveling word wall contains the same information as the class wall. The words students had written in are now typed in by you.

This process stays the same all year. On the first week of every month students get the new paper walls for their folders, and highlight the patterns and draw some of the visuals. They add words for the remainder of the month and the process gets repeated again.

Strategies & Activities for Language Arts

Independent Reading

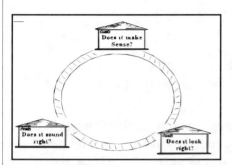

Another visual that works well in the traveling strategy folder is a railroad track with three train stations. Each station represents one of the cueing systems. Use of the three cueing systems needs to be a strategy that is explicitly taught. Tailor this train station to match your prompting language. Next to each train station write in the clues you give students when they are stuck. (See prompting language on pages 53-54).

Students can start at any station. This track continually goes by each station, or cueing system, and helps students to cross-check their responses.

Success at Home and School

Many students benefit from taking their traveling strategy folders home, but their folders don't usually make it back to school the next day. Give each child two folders, one stays at school and one goes home. This also helps strategies become consistent both at home and school.

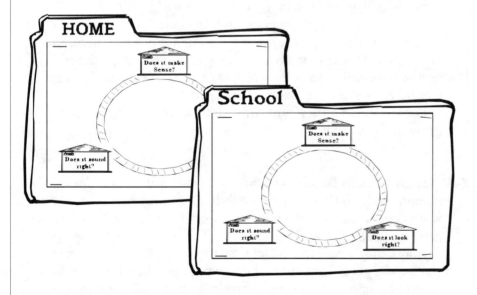

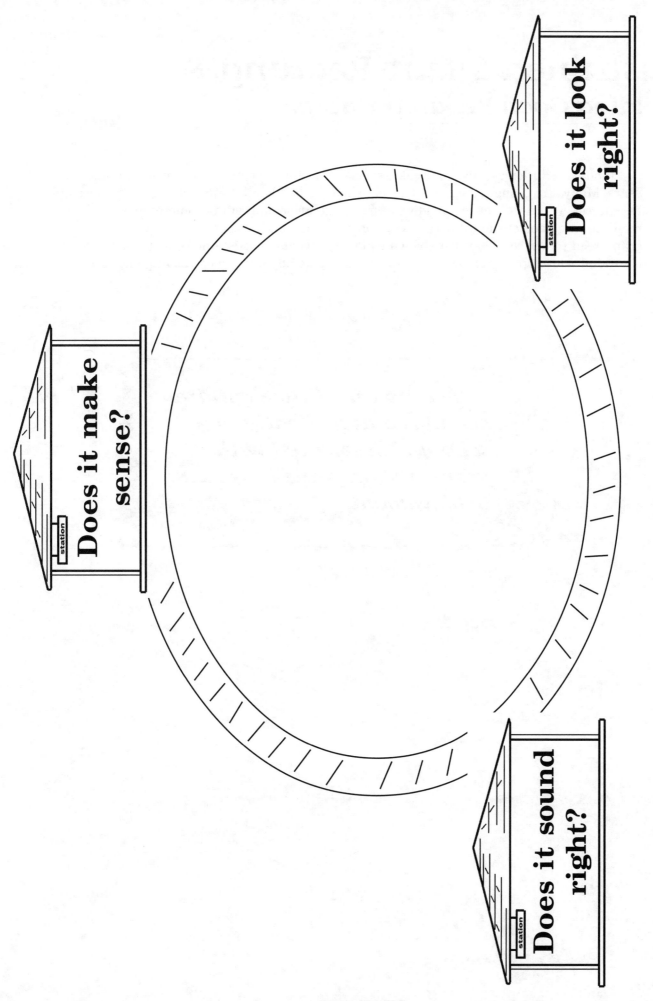

Sustained Silent Reading &
Building Good Reading Habits

Habits are difficult things to break, especially if they have been built over a number of years. Many struggling readers have established the bad habit of not setting themselves up for success. When they have a reading assignment, or begin reading something, they do not read the title, look at the pictures or captions, read the back jacket, or scan the last paragraph read yesterday. They just GO. One of the goals during sustained silent reading, in addition to developing the love of reading, is to create and build good reading habits.

"The amount of time children spend reading silently in school is associated with year-to-year gains in reading achievement."

Allington, 1984

✔ Before Reading

Each day, before and after students silent read, go through a process that helps students start to build the habit of setting themselves up for success: organizing before they begin. Have students get their books for SSR and go to the place where they will read. When they are ready to read, set the timer for one minute and tell students that nobody may begin reading. They must set themselves up. We want them to:

S.S.R
- 👁 Look at the pictures
- 👉 Point to the illustrations
- Flip through the book
- Read the BACK jacket
- Reread the last paragraph you read the previous day

 When the timer goes off, they may begin reading.

✔ After Reading

When SSR is over, many struggling readers just STOP. They stop reading, stop thinking, and stop reflecting. But when the act of reading is complete, a new phase of reading begins when the book is closed. This is the time when proficient readers reflect and think about the reading. Did they like it? Did it make sense?

To help students begin to think and reflect on their reading, follow the same process through when SSR is over as when it began. Set the timer for another minute and tell students they are not done reading yet. They need to reflect, to think about the book. Did they like it? Did they understand what was read? In the beginning you will need to model reflecting for your students. You can also pair students up to share with each other. They have one minute to tell their partner what they read about. When the timer goes off, set it for another minute and reverse roles — the talker is now the listener.

Writing

Young children may have a difficult time writing down their ideas because of a lack of sound and letter correspondence, or their thoughts are going faster than their ability to write them down. Older students may have difficulty sequencing, organizing ideas, and using detail. This section focuses on many strategies to help with difficulties in writing.

Writing

Boxes and Arrows

This is a great activity for students who are struggling in the following two areas:

1. Young emergent writers who struggle with **sounds and letters**. Boxes help students realize that pictures are a form of writing, and they can tell their stories and thoughts through pictures first, then work with the print.

2. Older students who have no difficulty writing but whose work just goes on and on with no **focus or connections.**

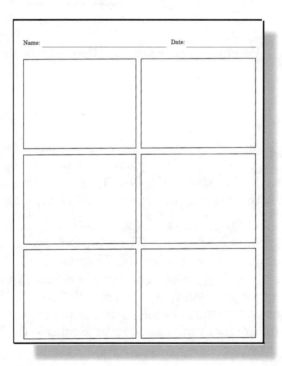

Name:_____ Date:_____

A Closer Look
A Real Life Classroom Example

Below is a sample from a first grade girl (Jo-Ann) who wanted to write about her birthday party. This sample was done together with the whole class in a modeling situation. Jo-Ann and the teacher were up at the board drawing the pictures together as Jo-Ann was telling the story. The rest of the class was watching and giving suggestions when Jo-Ann got stuck. (The regular print is what Jo-Ann said and the italicized print represents the group's suggestions.)

BOX 1 "I want to write a story about my birthday party. We had a lot of decorations." *"Why don't you draw some party hats to show the decorations."*

BOX 2 "Six people came to my party." *"Draw 6 people to show them."*

BOX 3 "I got lots of presents." *"Draw the presents."*

BOX 4 "We played lots of games. We played bobbing for apples and grab the donut . . ." (Jo-Ann was telling about the many games she played when one of her peers jumped in.) *"Just write the numbers 1-4 and then when you write tell about four games you played."* (The child then drew what is in the box for Jo-Ann.)

BOX 5 "Then everybody went home." *"Draw a house and say bye."*

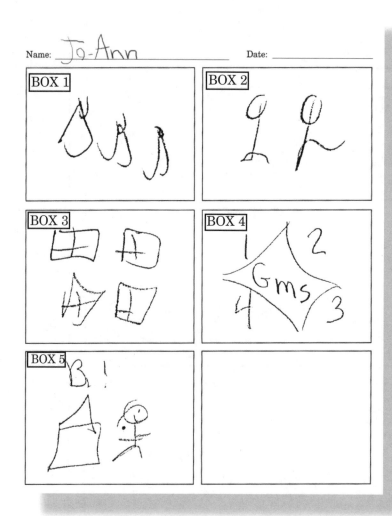

The next step is for Jo-Ann to take her boxes and glue or staple them onto the middle of a sheet of construction paper. She then writes just one letter to represent something from each box. Below is what she did.

(H for hats)

(P for presents)

(B for birthday)

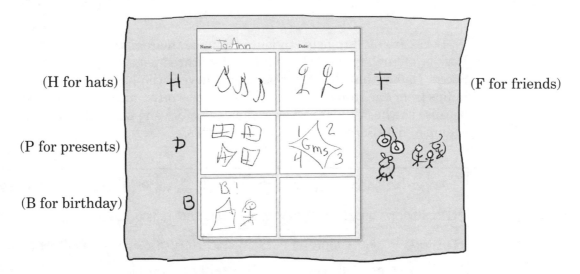

(F for friends)

When I read this story to her ... "Jo-Ann had a birthday party. She had a lot of decorations there. Six people came to her party..."

She looked at me and said "I didn't write that."

But she did! She wrote it in picture form.

Once students realize that pictures are writing, it is amazing how independent your emergent writers become when they use these boxes.

The next step, which might take weeks to get to, is for Jo-Ann to write a word that represents something from each box. The step after that, which may take another couple of weeks, is for her to write one sentence next to each box, and then two sentences, etc.

After she feels confident doing this, she can put the boxes over on the right hand of the large piece of paper and write on the left side. This helps her to see that writing is connected. You don't need to put one sentence next to each picture. All of the words can go together.

The final step is for Jo-Ann to draw the pictures, if she wants to, and then get a full sheet of paper and just write!

Strategies & Activities for Language Arts

A Closer Look
A Real Life Classroom Example

Boxes are used to help students organize their writing before they begin. Rose is a fourth grader who will turn in a three-page story titled "The Soccer Game," but the soccer game will never even begin in her story. She jumps from one thing to another. Her stories often make no sense at all because she hasn't planned or organized before she gets started. For example,"The Soccer Game" began like this:

"we had a soccer game after school, so when I went home from school mom made me lasagna. Lasagna is my favorite dinner. And as I was eating I looked outside and Jonathan, my neighbor, was playing frisbee with his dog. The frisbee was blue. You know blue is my favorite color, and my Uncle Tony has a blue truck and last year he got into an accident.....

Rose goes on and on and completely loses sense of what her story was going to be about.

On the right is an example of how she used the boxes. She calls this "arrows" because as she writes and includes the information in each box, she draws an arrow to the next event.

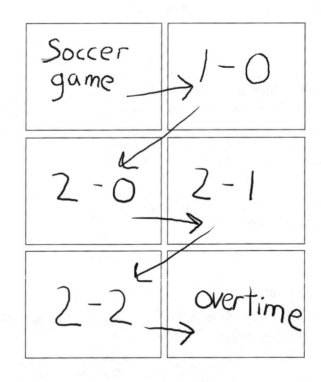

After Rose began calling this strategy arrows, some of the other students picked up on it. Trish remarked that she didn't need the boxes, all she needed was the arrows. She wrote:

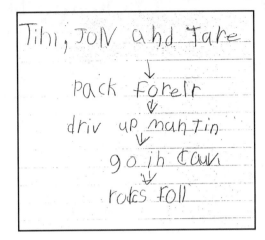

Tim, John and Terry

pack four-wheeler

drive up mountain

go in cave

rocks fall

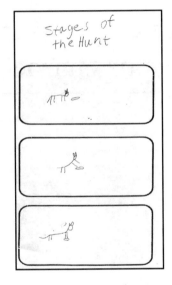 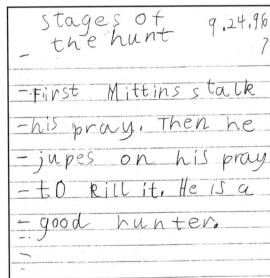

A younger child from Gahanna, Ohio completed this example

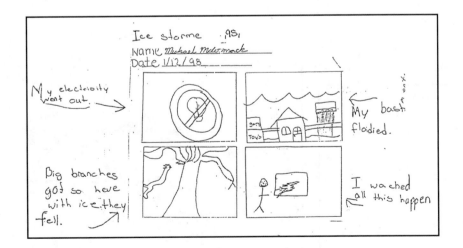

Michael McCormack, a student in Stacey Brandes' fourth grade, writes about the ice storms Burlington, Vermont was having in January 1998.

On pages 86 and 87 are two other reproducibles that my students have found very helpful. They use these forms either before they write to help them plan or after they have written to revise.

Character Development

Name: _____ Date: _____

Who? Appearance

Likes and Dislikes

Personality

Draw your character

Prove it

Setting Development

Name: _____ Date: _____

Where?

Describe it: Sight

Describe it: Sound

Describe it: Smell

Draw a picture of your setting

"Trust that your students want to be responsible, successful learners. Sometimes they forget."

Esther Wright
Loving Discipline A to Z

Part 3
Strategies & Activities
Across the Curriculum

Strategies & Activities
Across the Curriculum

Students make gains when strategies are consistent. It is better for students to have a limited number of activities and strategies that they use well, rather than have a wealth of them which are applied poorly or not at all.

This part of the book will focus on five strategies. These ideas can be used in all areas of the curriculum, and will help students break tasks down and organize them into manageable pieces. The five strategies and how they will aid students are listed below.

- **Flipbooks** help students organize their thinking and learning.

- **Highlighting Tape** allows students to manipulate text and the skills found in the text.

- **Webs** help students brainstorm and organize information before they start any writing activity.

- **Scripts** are written sets of directions and information that students can refer to when they get stuck.

- **Graphic Organizers and Structured Overviews** help students organize information, form connections, and have some prior knowledge. They offer students a place to go when they are confused.

How to Make a Flipbook

STEP 1: Take a sheet of 12" x 18" paper and fold in half lengthwise.

STEP 2: Cut the **top** piece to make two, three, or four flaps. Do not cut through both sides.

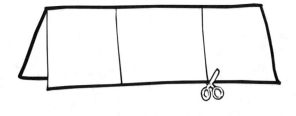

Three–flap flipbook

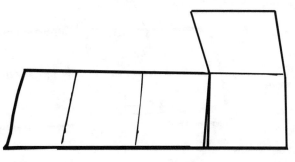

Four–flap flipbook

A Closer Look
A Real Life Classroom Example

A Sample Four-Day Lesson Plan
Making a flipbook seems so easy, but it takes about a week to introduce.

✓ ## Day 1
Objective: Students learn what a flipbook is and how they can use it.

Give the flipbooks, already made, to your students and just brainstorm what they are and what they could be used for. All of the ideas are put onto a chart. Some different names students called them are: flipbooks, flapbooks, liftbooks. The goal for day one is to get students thinking about using both the outside and inside flaps for pieces of information.

Some ideas younger students came up with:

The letter M
Melinda's idea was to use the flipbook with the letter M. Write M on the four flaps. Under the flaps she said you could: Practice writing the letter M, draw pictures of things that begin with M, glue magazine pictures of words that contain the letter M, and copy words from charts in the room that contain the letter M.

Shapes
Theresa's idea was to use the flipbook with shapes. She wrote the names of four shapes on the outside flaps: circle, square, triangle, and rectangle. Under the flaps she drew pictures of the shapes and then she drew pictures of things in the classroom that have that shape.

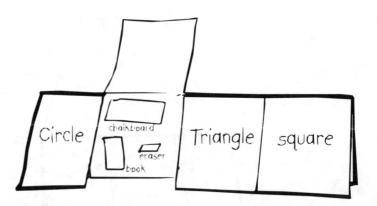

Some ideas older students came up with:

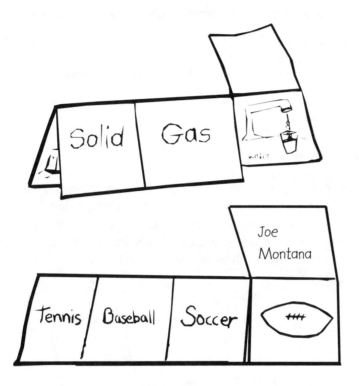

Solid, Liquid, Gas
Diana's idea was to use a flipbook with her science unit. She told the class we needed only three flaps. She gave examples of each state of matter under the flaps.

Sports
Carmine's idea was to write the names of sports on the outside flaps and the names of players and pictures of sports equipment on the inside flaps.

 Day 2

Objective: Students learn how to make flipbooks.

Students get a full sheet of paper and are taught how to make a flipbook. Brainstorm all the potential problems. What can you do if you: fold the paper so it is crooked? cut through both pieces of paper? the paper rips?, etc. If students know what problems might come up, and have solutions before facing those problems, then the greater their independence.

Again you might brainstorm ideas that can be used with flipbooks.

The Farm
Ken's idea was to use his flipbook to show all the different things you might see on a farm. He gave categories on the outside flaps and details on the inside.

Strategies & Activities Across the Curriculum

Day 3
Objective: Students can make and use flipbooks independently.

Students are given an assignment. They have to make a flipbook and then do something with it. The goal is to have them make the book independently and then come up with an idea to use with it. The biggest problem this day is summarized in the following dialogue:

Student: "What do you want me to do with the flipbook?"
Teacher: "Anything you want to do."
Student: "Yeah, but what do *you* want me to do?"

Students want us to tell them what to do. You can now refer them to the chart displayed from Day 1. We want our students to be able to work independently. Tie nothing curriculum based into the assignment yet. Once students know they can follow these directions easily, then it's time to tie in the skills. At this point, then, all of their energy and effort goes into the utilization and application of the skill, not in the making and following directions for a flipbook.

Family of Facts
Dana used her flipbook to organize her family of facts. She wrote a number on the outside of each flap. On the inside she wrote the four equations that made up the family of facts.

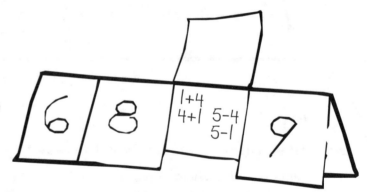

Quotation Marks
Carol used her flipbook to intergrate the language arts curriculum (quotation marks) and the science curriculum (predator & prey). On the outside flaps she drew a picture of a predator. On the inside flaps she wrote what that predator would say and drew a picture of its prey.

Day 4

Objective: Students use the flipbooks with current curriculum.

Now assign the flipbook according to a part of your curriculum. Whatever you are teaching at this point, assign it with a flipbook. The following are some examples of how to tie this into various curriculum areas.

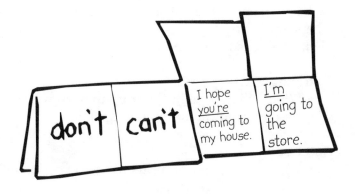

Contractions

Stacie and Matthew used flipbooks with contractions. Stacie wrote one contraction on the outside of each flap and then under the flaps used the contraction in a sentence.

Matthew used the outside flaps to categorize the spellings of contractions, and under each flap listed all of the contractions that fit that pattern.

New England States

Carol cut her flipbook into six parts instead of four. She wrote the New England states she was learning about on the outside flaps. On the inside she wrote the capital, state bird, state flag, and she drew a picture of the state flower.

Strategies & Activities Across the Curriculum

Predictions

Students often give predictions that make no sense at all. They have not followed through or analyzed thoughts and opinions as to whether they have made a good prediction or not. Little or no evidence is given to back up opinions or predictions.

Flipbooks help students follow through on their thoughts. They help students think about why they feel certain things will happen. There are many different kinds of predictions students are asked to complete.

Language Arts
- What will happen in the story tomorrow?
- Predict what could/would happen if ...

Science
- What could happen in this science experiment?

Social Studies
- Predict what might have happened if a certain event didn't take place.

Math
- Predict the area, perimeter, weight, measure, time, etc.
- Predict how long it would take to drive from point A to point B.

Turn the flipbooks around (the uncut side is now on top and the flaps are on the bottom). Begin with the side that is not cut.

On the top piece students write their prediction. On each of the bottom flaps students write one reason WHY they wrote that prediction. This gets students to back up their responses and opinions. It forces them to follow through with their thinking.

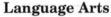

Write Prediction here

Sequencing

Sequencing is an important skill that is utilized in all areas of the curriculum. Children are often asked to:

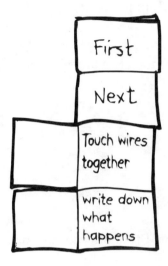

- follow a set of steps to perform a science experiment
- sequence a story
- use a formula (involving a sequence of steps) to solve a math problem

When older students have science experiments to do, or projects that involve certain steps, some just start without thinking about the order of the tasks, or about what really needs to be done. They leave out parts and then the end result/conclusion is incorrect.

Step-by-Step

Flipbooks help students organize information by having them break it into smaller chunks. When working with following directions or steps in a process, flaps can be labeled first through last or first through fourth. Any time my students have an assignment that involves sequencing or steps in a process they must fill out a flipbook. The goal is to get students to write down step-by-step directions in their own words in the flipbook. Sometimes students dictate to me and I will do the writing. If a group of students is working together the group has to make a flipbook and show it to me before they get started.

When sequencing stories, it helps students look for major events and plot incidents. Flaps can be labeled beginning, middle, and end.

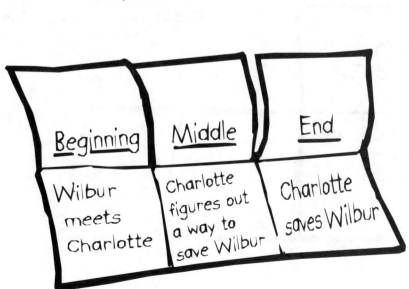

Word Problems

Many times students just begin writing word problems without planning, so the problem makes no sense at all. Also, students are often confused about whether to add or subtract.

Each word problem students write will have three steps:

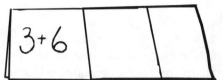

STEP 1: First have students write any equation on the top flap.

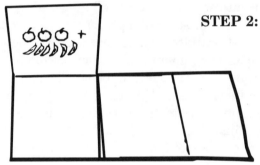

STEP 2: Open up the flap. Students can now draw the equation.

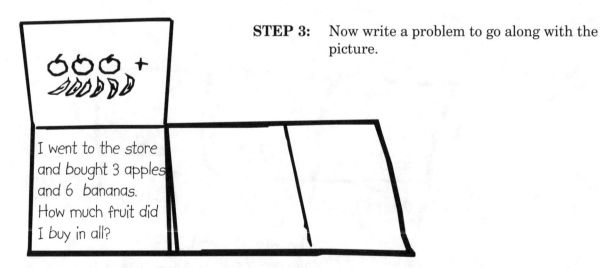

STEP 3: Now write a problem to go along with the picture.

I went to the store and bought 3 apples and 6 bananas. How much fruit did I buy in all?

Descriptive Questions

When responding to descriptive requests such as,

Describe your character

Describe a dessert

Describe the book you are reading,

students often give a three word sentence: "He is nice. It is good." When asked to add more they will add the words *very* or *really*: "He is *very* nice." "It is *really* good." There is little evidence given to prove or back up responses.

Flipbooks help students to key in on two-to-four words that describe. Flipbooks also help students provide details and examples to support what they write. It also helps them to add more details and organize. For example, when describing James from Roald Dahl's book, *James and the Giant Peach*, the outside of the flipbook might look like this:

Under each flap students need to prove what they said on the outside flap. They have to back up their opinion or answer with evidence from the book. They can write words, phrases, or page numbers from the book that shows an action or something that was said on that specific page. They can also draw pictures, make webs, etc. The inside might look like this:

After completing a flipbook, the next step, depending on ability, would be to take the information that is now organized and put it into a paragraph or a piece of writing.

A Closer Look
A Real Life Classroom Example

My fourth grade students were given an assignment. The assignment was to describe the book they were reading. They could tell about anything.

Below is a piece of writing from that assignment.

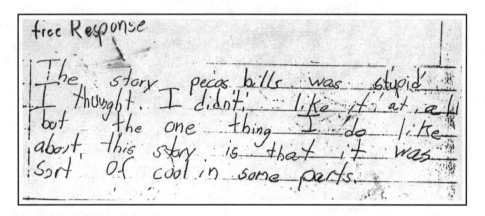

free Response

The story I pecas bills was stupid I thought. I didnt like it at all but the one thing I do like about this story is that it was sort of cool in some parts.

Did this student (Tina) really read the book? Did she understand what she read? It is very difficult to answer these questions by just reading her paper. Tina did not make a flipbook before she wrote. Tina got this paper back the next day and was told she had to redo it because she gave no details or evidence to prove what was written. Her assignment now was to make a flipbook first and then do her rewrite.

Tina now made a flipbook with three flaps labeled:

Stupid   didn't like it at all   Sort of cool

This is the written piece she turned in the next day.

> The story Pecas bill was stupid because it was so out outrageous like the part (where) Bill can only talk in wolves language. I don't like this story at all because I don't Tall Tales. The only one part I do like was when Pecas Bill grew up with the wolves.

I never assign flipbooks with descriptive questions until there is a problem. I highly recommend that students make a flipbook first, but I don't make it a requirement. Most students who struggle see anything that involves a piece of paper and a pencil as work. They are already struggling and now they are given another activity, a flipbook, in addition to the assignment. Students need to see that the flipbooks make the assignment easier, not harder. So do not assign it until a child needs to redo a paper or has turned something in that is unacceptable. Once students see that flipbooks do make the work easier, more organized, and may prevent them from having to redo work, you will see them choosing to make the flipbooks on their own.

Strategies & Activities Across the Curriculum

Vocabulary Development

When students have a difficult time understanding new vocabulary and concepts, they often memorize words for tests or units and then forget them. There is no carry over into daily written work or into the child's speaking vocabulary.

Flipbooks help students make connections between the unknown and the known. Flipbooks connect vocabulary and concepts to meaningful experiences in a child's life.

There are two ways flipbooks can be used for vocabulary development. One way is to write down the vocabulary word on the outside flaps. The student will write the same word four times. On the inside flaps the student can do the following:

Under flap 1:
Write down synonyms.

Under flap 2:
Write down antonyms.

Under flap 3:
Use the word in a sentence about home, school, or you.

Under flap 4:
Find the definition in a dictionary or a glossary and write it down. THEN, the child must write down one more definition of the word in his own words, not the glossary or dictionary definition.

Another way to use these is to have a different word on each flap. Under the flaps students can do all or some of the above for each word.

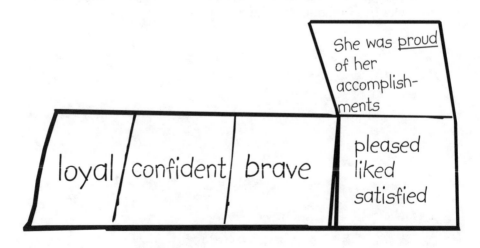

Highlighting Tape

Highlighting tape is a tape that works just like a highlighter. It can be reused over and over again and will not ruin your books. It comes in two sizes, wide (1 7/8") and narrow (9/16"). Two large rolls, at about $6.50 each, is all you will need for the whole year. For easy management, cut the tape into strips and put four to five pieces of it on strips of oaktag. It is available from Crystal Springs Books (1-800-321-0401). This tape can be used in a variety of ways to help students focus on and manipulate text.

Wikki Stix can be used for any of the following activities, and are available from Crystal Springs Books. Pipe cleaners and pieces of colored overheads can also be used. The only difference is that because these two materials are not sticky like highlighting tape and *Wikki Stix* you can only work with one page, not the whole book, at a time (pieces would fall off as you turned the pages).

Highlighting Tape

READING AND WRITING

Highlighting tape helps students find and focus on the skills embedded in real reading and writing contexts.

Print Concepts

Highlighting tape can be used with morning messages, classroom news charts, big books, and posters. After reading the texts, students highlight a letter, word, or sentence. This helps students see the differences between these three concepts.

Sight Words

The key to students grasping sight words is multiple exposure. They need to find them, read them, write them, and highlight them over and over. The tape is a great resource for this. If you are concentrating on the words "the" and "said," students' independent work assignment is to take the tape and find those words as many times as they can in their reading books.

Most of the time the size of the tape is not a perfect match to the word or letter the child is working with. To remedy this problem, take a black marker and draw an oval on the piece of tape. It is much easier for the child to focus now. If the child holds the tape horizontally, the oval is big enough to ring a word. If the tape is held vertically, it is skinny enough to ring just one letter.

Strategies & Activities Across the Curriculum

Writing Difficulties (Fine Motor)

Students who have fine motor difficulties love the highlighting tape. Instead of having to write, they can just highlight the answers. For example, instead of:

- writing definitions,
   they can highlight the definitions;

- writing sentences and circling the verbs,
   they can highlight verbs in their book;

- describing their character,
   they can highlight places in the book where it
   tells about their character.

Play with Print

My students and I have organized the books in our library so they can actually play with the print. On the left front page of each book in our classroom library, we write the word(s), letter(s), or skill(s) that the student will be able to find a number of times in the book. On the right page we put a pocket that holds a strip(s) of oaktag with the highlighting tape.

I organize the books for these activities during reading groups *with* my students. Don't set up the books without your students. Organizing books this way provides powerful mini-lessons.

The student takes the highlighting tape and highlights that word, letter, or skill every time he sees it in the book. You can have students focus on just about anything. For example, highlight:

- all the words that are plural
- words that have a long /a/ sound
- all the quotation marks
- verbs that end in "ing"
- the letter F

- all the verbs
- all the nouns
- the word SAID
- the word THE

At the left is an example of what the inside of a book might look like. On the top left is the skill that the book is loaded with and what the student needs to highlight and focus on. On the bottom left is an envelope that contains the card found on page 105.

I found _____ times.

Name _____

I found _____ times.

Name _____

I found _____ times.

Name _____

I found _____ times.

Name _____

A Closer Look
A Real Life Classroom Example

Coordinate Higlighting Tape with Flipbooks

After students finish highlighting, they need to fill out the card found in the envelope. They need to count the number of highlighted items they found and fill in that information.

In this example, Leann was looking for specific sight words. She held the flipbook vertically so the flaps opened to the left.

On the outside she wrote the words she was looking for.

On the inside she used each word in a sentence.

outside   *inside*

In this example, Kevin is looking for specific letters. He held the paper horizontally so the flaps open up.

He drew pictures, wrote words and sentences that went along with the letters.

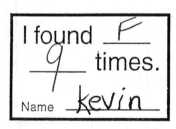

outside

inside

Highlighting Tape

INFERENCING

When students say, "The answer is not there," it is usually because the question is an inferential one and the answer is inbetween the lines. Most often students look for the answer to an inferential question as if it were a literal question, expecting the answer to be right there, which it is not.

It's Inbetween the Lines

When students are having a difficult time answering inferential questions, the teacher can take the highlighting tape and mark the section that contains the answer and say, "The answer is somewhere inbetween these lines." It gives students a place to focus.

Homework Helper

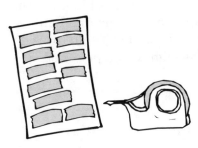

When older students have homework that contains questions to be answered, you can highlight paragraphs or pieces of text that contain the answers. It makes the task a little less overwhelming. Also, if students cannot answer a question, they can't just leave it blank and say they were stuck. They need to highlight a passage that they think might help or contain the answer.

Strategies & Activities Across the Curriculum

Highlighting Tape

PREVIEWING

Highlighting tape works well for previewing science and social studies texts for older students, and picture and word walks for younger students.

Previewing Text (for older students)

Before students begin reading any science or social studies text, they must preview the chapter, unit, or section to be read. They need to highlight the title, bold-faced print words, vocabulary words, definitions, pictures, captions, graphs, etc. These are the concepts you will focus on during pre-reading.

Prepare for Tests

While you are reading in a textbook, if there is an important piece of information, have students highlight the sentence or paragraph. I will often have them highlight something that will be on a test. When they begin to study for the test they can focus on the highlighted pieces of information.

Picture and Word Walks (for younger students)

The tape is a great tool to use for picture walks and word walks during guided reading. Before reading a book, students are asked to flip through the book looking at pictures and finding words they know. Give each of your students a strip of oaktag that contains pieces of highlighting tape. Ask them to highlight the word **THE** three times on a certain page. You can ask them to highlight the funny part of the picture, or highlight the part of the picture that shows a character is very happy.

Webs

Webs are helpful in many curriculum areas. They help students brainstorm and organize information *before* they start any kind of writing activity. They help students break down and organize new information so it makes sense. Webs also help students make connections. This section will explore three different kinds of webs: sense webs, question webs, and student generated webs.

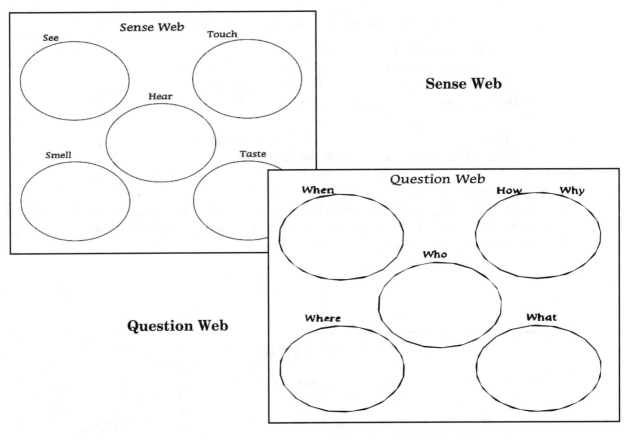

Sense Web

Question Web

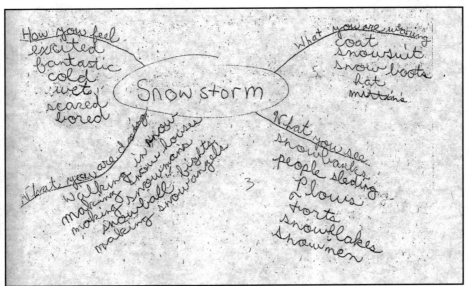

Student Generated Web

Strategies & Activities Across the Curriculum

Sense Webs

Sense Webs help students get detail into their writing by asking them to reflect and focus on the five senses. Students respond to the following questions:

- What would you see?
- What would you hear?
- What would you smell?
- What would you feel?
- What would you taste?

Some examples of how to use sense webs across your curriculum include:

- Pretend you were a piece of seaweed.
- Pretend you were a carnivorous dinosaur.
- Describe a setting in your creative writing piece.
- Describe the setting in the book you are reading.
- Where is your favorite place to be?
- Choose a person from history and describe a day in his life.
- Pretend you were a pilgrim on the Mayflower.

Below is a sample of a sense web that a group of students and I worked on when we were comparing a city and a country. We split the ovals in half so we could work with both concepts in the same circle.

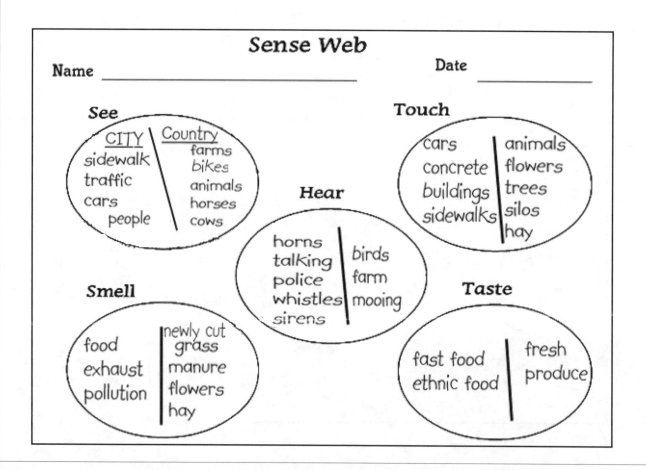

Sense Web

Name _____ Date _____

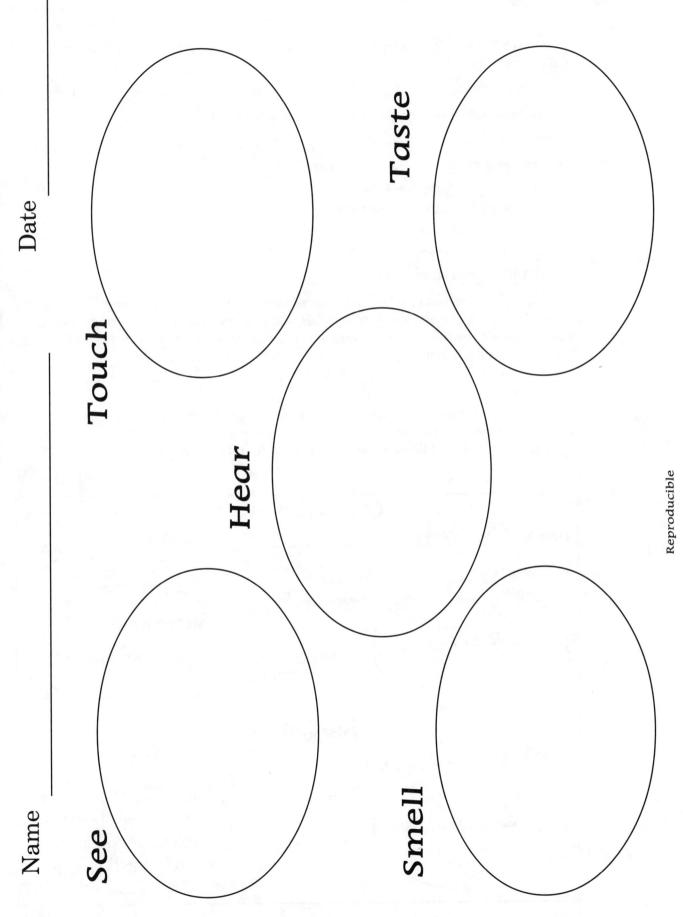

Touch

See

Hear

Taste

Smell

QuestionWebs help students organize and add more detail to their writing by reflecting and focusing on the six question words:

Who   What   Where   Why   When   How

Here are examples of how to use question webs across your curriculum:

- Write about a certain time in history.
- Write about a certain place in history.
- Any creative writing assignment.
  - The happiest time in your life.
  - The saddest time in your life.
  - Your summer vacation.
  - Child's own story ideas.

The question web can also be used to summarize books and/or a chapter in a book. You can use this web orally as a quick comprehension check with students during reading group. It can also be filled in as a pre-reading activity to set prior knowledge and set the stage before students read.

Below is an example of how this was used with a fourth grade social studies unit. Students were responsible for researching the origins of the American Flag. Richard used a question web and filled in each circle as he found the information.

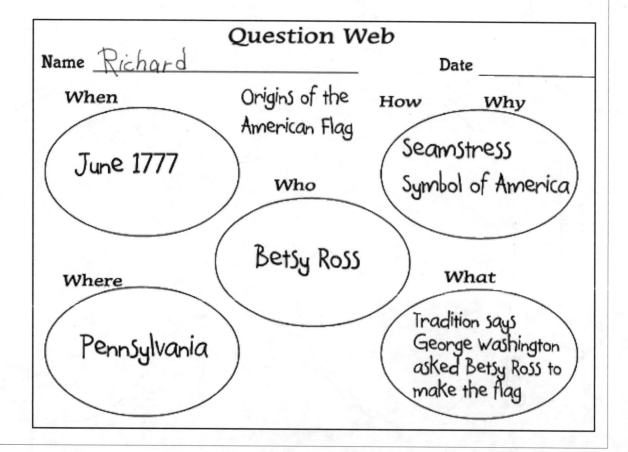

Question Web

Name _____

Date _____

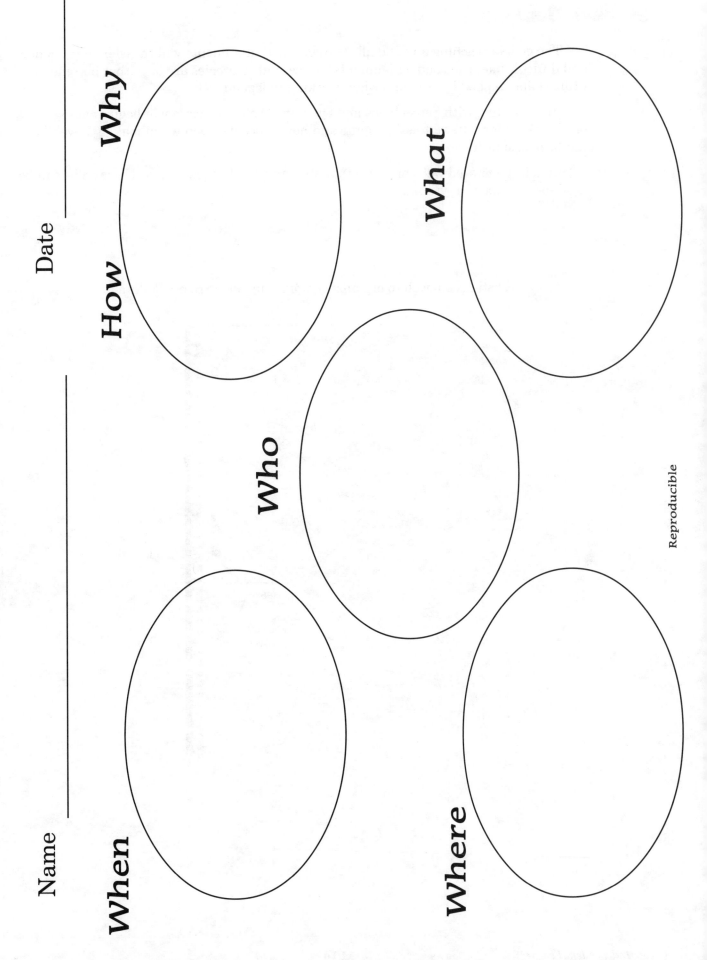

Why

How

What

Who

When

Where

The goal of teaching any and all strategies is that students will transfer them to new and difficult materials and assignments. Successful strategies are ones that become utilized and applied by students when working independently.

After working with Sense Webs and Question Webs, students will begin making webs on their own for different assignments and new concepts, even when making a web has not been assigned!

Student generated webs are ones that students create themselves. These webs can be used for just about anything.

Kristi used a web to organize a biography about Ben Franklin.

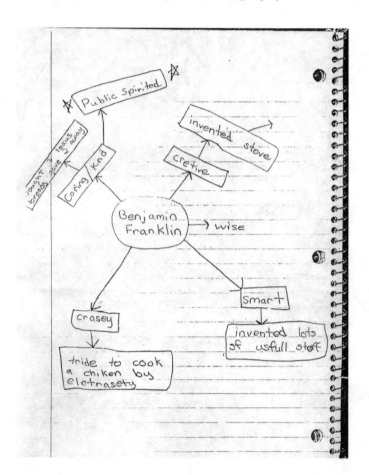

Paul generated his own sense web to describe his favorite place.

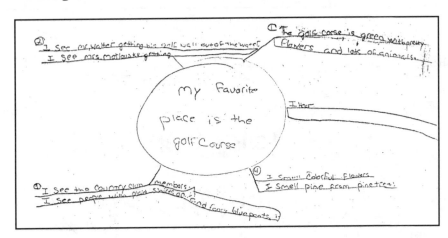

Alisha used a web to help her organize a creative writing piece taking place during a snowstorm.

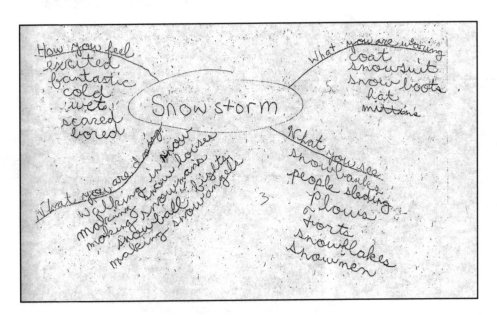

Janine used a web to organize a persuasive writing piece.

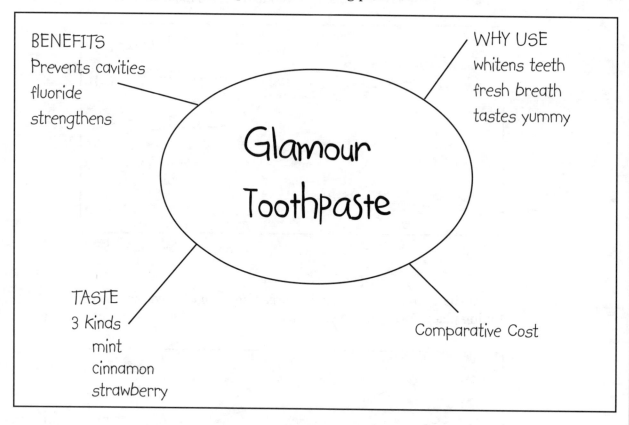

A first grade teacher created this web with her students at the beginning of a unit on bears to find out what information they wanted to learn.

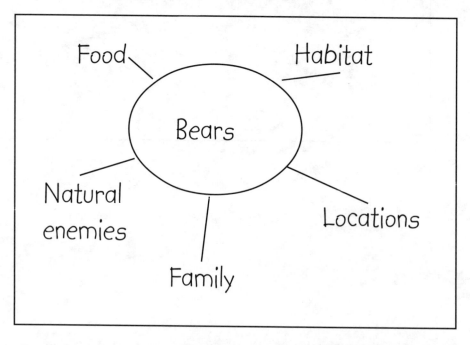

Help Students Transfer from Webs to Writing

The biggest problem for students is not the web itself. They generally do very well organizing and setting up the webs. It is the transition from the web to the actual piece of writing that is difficult for them.

Setting up a form that shows students how to go from the web to writing has been very successful. It is important to set up the steps on how to go from the web to an actual piece of writing with your students. After creating the steps, make a form together to help students remember the steps.

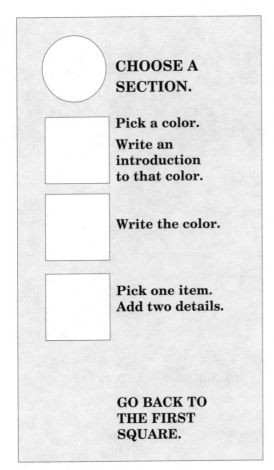

This form is what students made to help them through the transition from webs to the writing process. Every child gets a copy of the form on the left. This form was created by my students. Your form might look different depending on the way your students set it up.

The shapes on the left are place holders so students don't lose their place. They put a pen cap or eraser in the shape as they are doing that activity and then move it to the next shape when they are ready to do the next step.

The first shape (circle) is different because that shape corresponds to the section that students are working on. The next three shapes are the same (squares) because students continually go from the first square to the last square until they finish working with a specific section.

The next two pages explain how my students used this form to help them transition from a web to a piece of writing.

A Closer Look
A Real Life Classroom Example

Below is a sample of an older child's web for his autobiography. The following page describes the process Oliver went through when transitioning from a web to his writing.

STEP 1

Number each section. Each section will become a paragraph. (Notice how Oliver changed his mind between paragraphs 4 and 5.)

STEP 2

Oliver chose one section of his web to work with. He categorized all the words in each section by circling the words that fit together using colored pencils.

Oliver circled:
dog, cat, fish, and kittens in red because those are animals in his house;

rabbits and horse in blue because they are in the barn;

frogs and skunk in yellow because they are outside.

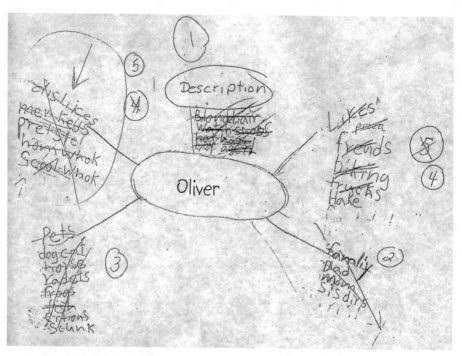

Oliver's categories are:

1) Description
blond hair
watch
shoes
hat
hazel eyes
boy
age 11

2) Family
dad
mom
sisters

3) Pets
dog
cat
horse
rabbits
frogs
fish
kittens
skunk

4) Likes
pizza
friends
biking
trucks
hockey

5) Dislikes
mean kids
pretzels
homework
schoolwork

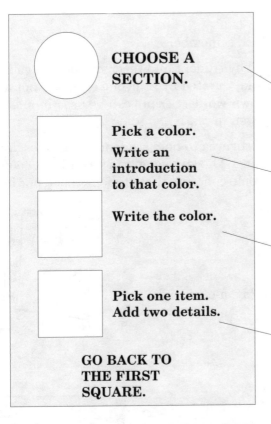

CHOOSE A SECTION.

Pick a color.

Write an introduction to that color.

Write the color.

Pick one item. Add two details.

GO BACK TO THE FIRST SQUARE.

CHOOSE A SECTION.

Pick a color.

Write an introduction to that color.

Write the color.

Pick one item. Add two details.

GO BACK TO THE FIRST SQUARE.

STEP 3

Oliver used this form to write about each section.

First he chose the "pet" section, number 3.

He chose the words he circled in red and wrote:
I have some animals that live in my house.
They are a dog, a cat, some fish and some kittens. (He crosses out each piece of information in his web as he includes it.)

He picked the word "kitten." *My cat just had five kittens. They are 3 weeks old now.*

STEP 4

Oliver went back to the first square and chose another color. He continued to use the squares until he had used all the colors in that section.

Oliver went back to the circle and chose a new section. He chose the "likes" section, number 4. This is what he wrote:

I have some favorite foods.
I like pizza and hot dogs.
I love pepperoni on my pizza.
We always get it from Connie's Pizza Kitchen.

Notice how Oliver added hot dogs as he wrote. I often see students adding new information when they use this form.

Strategies & Activities Across the Curriculum

Scripts

Scripts are written sets of directions and information that students can refer to when they get stuck. Scripts can be an excellent resource to help students access:

- steps in a process
- procedures
- information that they may not be able to remember

It is imperative that the scripts be created by student and teacher, not the teacher alone. If students are just given a script already created by someone else, it is not as effective or efficient as when they use their own words. Scripts can be used in most areas of the curriculum. They work exceptionally well in math.

Scripts can also be used in the language arts area to help students with rules and concepts that they have difficulty remembering. The language arts script book could be set up the same way as the math script book. Some concepts that students have put into their scripts include:

- plural rules
- rules for adding -ed and -ing endings
- most commonly misspelled words
- subject and predicates
- different spellings for the same sound (ay, a-e, ai, eigh)

Math Scripts

Creating a Script

STEP 1

Choose a concept that is difficult for students, for example, rounding off.

STEP 2

While working through a problem together, the student and teacher discuss how to write step-by-step instructions for solving the problem. Write a set of rough draft directions together.

STEP 3

Using the rough draft directions, put a square or circle next to each step as a place holder for students so they do not forget which step they are on or what needs to be done next.

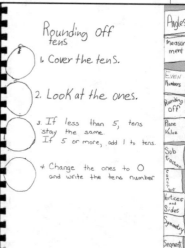

STEP 4

Using the script, have students practice doing some problems to see if the the directions are clear and easy to follow. This is where the script might need to be revised. The child should be able to use the script alone, with no teacher direction.

STEP 5

After using the script for a couple of days, and rewriting anything that needs clarification, students then write the final copy themselves into their own script book.

Make a Script Book

There are two different ways the script book can be set up. The first way is for students to use a spiral notebook or composition book. Students put masking tape tabs on it as they add new scripts.

— Rounding off to 10

— Rounding off to 100

— Symmetry

— Odd/Even

Make a Script Folder

The second way to organize scripts is with a file folder. The student writes the title "Math Scripts" and decorates the outside of the folder. On the inside of the folder, on the top right side, are two brad fasteners that hold all of the scripts. On the left side are the list of scripts that have been completed. Students can put page numbers next to each item.

A Closer Look
A Real Life Classroom Example

Here are examples of scripts created and used in the math area by Phyllis, a fourth grade student.

The circles on the left side of the book represent Phyllis' place holders.

Phyllis organized her scripts by using a composition book and masking tape tabs. She labeled her tabs:

>   Angles
>   Measurement
>   Even numbers
>   Rounding off
>   Place Value
>   Subtraction
>   Congruent
>   Vertical and sides
>   Symmetry
>   Segment

Notice how Phyllis wrote out the first two steps numbers one and two. She then got very tired and the teacher wrote the other steps for her.

If the math concept does not have certain steps or a procedure to follow, then no place holders are used.

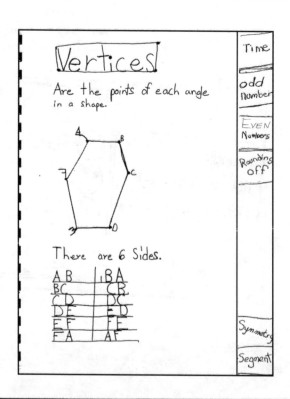

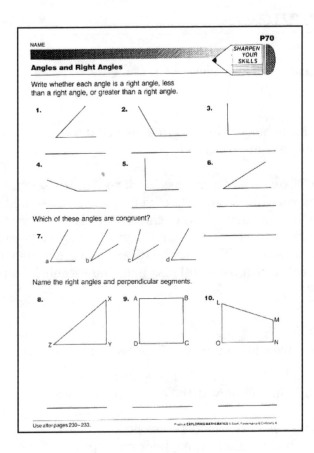

This is a page from Phyllis' fourth grade math book (*Scott Foresman and Company*). When she got to this page she immediately yelled, "I can't do this. I don't know what a right triangle is." She then said, "Oops, I can use my script book."

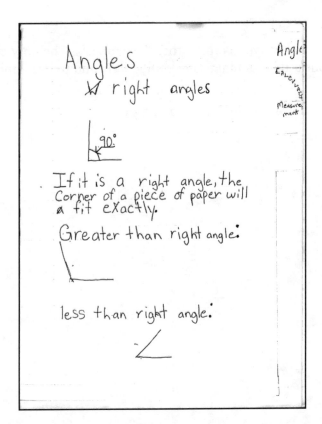

This is the page that Phyllis referred to in order to independently complete problems 1-6 in her workbook.

Strategies & Activities Across the Curriculum

Graphic Organizers
& Structured Overviews

Graphic Organizers and Structured Overviews help students:

- organize information
- form connections
- have some prior knowledge before they begin a new chapter
- have a place to go when they are confused

Graphic Organizers and Structured Overviews work well in the science and social studies areas. The ideas and concepts from each of your units is presented to students in the form of an organizer before any discussion of the unit begins. These organizers introduce the key concepts, how the concepts relate, and new vocabulary. They also give an overview of the entire unit or chapter. They can be referred to any time students are working with the content area. Organizers will also help you establish your goals and expectations for the unit.

Organize Your Goals

To begin creating an organizer for your unit of study, think about the following:

- What are the main ideas I want to stress in this unit?
- What do I want my students to know at the end of the chapter?
- What is the key vocabulary?
- How does the vocabulary relate to the key concepts?
- How can I organize this information into a diagram or picture form that shows the relationships?

There are no right or wrong ways to create these organizers. The only criterion is that the organizer will help your students make the connections and understand the concepts more easily.

On the following page is an example of an organizer.

Give each student a copy of the organizer and "walk" them through the information. Point out the relationships and key vocabulary you have included. Students will not have mastery at this time but they will have the "framework" that gives them an understanding of all the information that will be learned.

When students look at the tree organizer below, the first thing they notice is the two different types of trees. We point out the new vocabulary, (conifers and deciduous), but it is the pictures at this point that are meaningful. Students also know they will be learning about the products we get from trees.

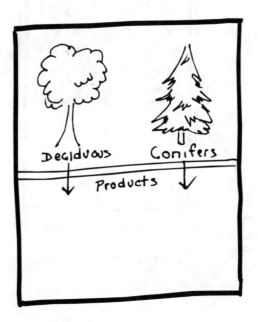

Use your organizers to brainstorm about concepts and elicit prior knowledge before you begin teaching.

How Students Use the Organizers

Have each student glue his organizer onto the middle of a piece of 12" x 18" construction paper. This paper is used throughout the teaching of the whole unit or chapter. The two sides can be folded in so that it fits into a notebook or pocket folder.

Students can write a number of things on the organizer to help with understanding:

draw pictures

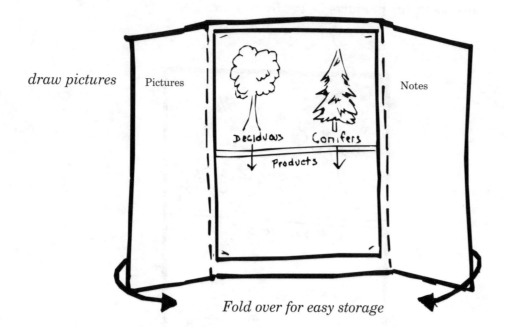

take notes

write page numbers where that specific information can be found

Fold over for easy storage

Every time you are working with this unit, students must have their organizer on their desk to refer to and add information to.

A List of Vocabulary and Information

At the beginning of each unit give students a piece of paper with a list of all of the new vocabulary and pieces of information they will be learning. This list organizes curriculum in the order that you will be teaching, from the bottom of the paper to the top of the paper. This list should be double spaced. As students learn the new information, they cut it out and glue it onto their organizer where it belongs.

This is an example of a list that students might receive for the science unit about trees. Your curriculum will dictate what is put on the list. Your list might be one or two pages long depending on how much information students will be learning.

lose leaves in fall

seeds

pine cones   oak

acorns   maple

wood   elm

paper   evergreen

maple syrup

fruit

Students cut out and glue the vocabulary and information onto their graphic organizers.

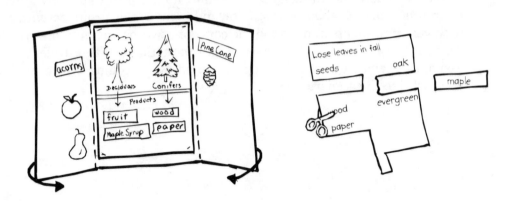

Students have remarked that it is much easier to remember facts and information when they use graphic organizers because they can visualize the webs, pictures, etc.

Using These Activities & Strategies
within the Context of a Diverse Classroom

Independent work time is often the most difficult activity to manage in a classroom. Students seem to constantly form a line at our desks and we rarely get through a reading group without being interrupted every two minutes. After a specific assignment is given a workbook page, for example, many problems immediately creep up:

- Tina can't read the directions or the sentences on the page.
- Dana gets done in two minutes and announces, "I'm done now. What do I do?"
- Cathi is only half way through the page when the period is over.
- Phyllis just fills in all the blanks without reading the directions and the whole paper is done incorrectly, and in a rush.
- Alisha is saying, "I don't get it. I don't understand the directions."
- Jack is copying his neighbor's paper.

AND, the children that have been taken for a reading group have been sitting for ten minutes while we try to take care of the line that has formed and address all of the above problems.

HELP!

There is never the perfect assignment. It is always too hard for some, too easy for others.

There are students who are done in minutes, asking, "Now what do I do?" There are students who need two days to do the same assignment.

This is where the difficulty lies for educators. For example, my fourth grade classroom was learning about verbs. They did many whole group activities and mini-lessons with verbs. Students understood the concept of verbs and action words, but now it came time for the assignment. This was a nightmare. Some of the students finished the assignment while it was still being explained. Some couldn't even read the directions. It was just like the scenario above.

Let Students Show What They Know

Think about assigning independent work and giving assignments to students in a way that reaches all their needs and levels, as well as supports your curriculum.

Students are given the curriculum, skill, or concept that you want them to work with. Their assignment is basically *show what you know*. They can do anything they choose. The activities and strategies from Part 3: *Strategies Across the Curriculum* in this book are now used. We have a chart in the room that looks like this:

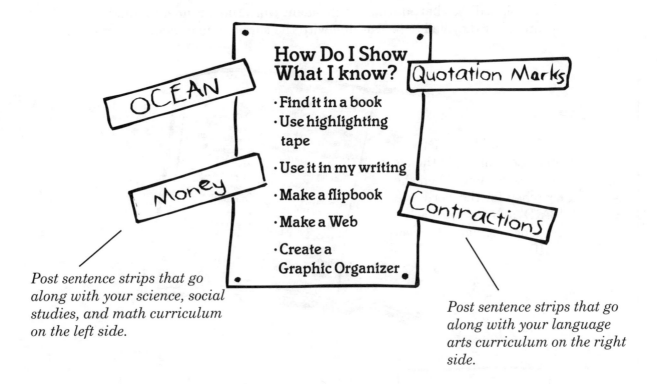

How Do I Show What I know?
- Find it in a book
- Use highlighting tape
- Use it in my writing
- Make a flipbook
- Make a Web
- Create a Graphic Organizer

Post sentence strips that go along with your science, social studies, and math curriculum on the left side.

Post sentence strips that go along with your language arts curriculum on the right side.

The activities that are on the chart remain the same. What changes are sentence strips that are put up on the sides to coordinate with your curriculum.

Two Ways to Use This Chart

This chart can be the work or it can be what students do when they are finished with their assignments. If the chart is the work then usually students have a time span on which they need to be working with application and utilization of the skill. For example, students may have 30 minutes to show what they know about contractions. Some will get one thing done, others may get two activities completed.

If used as a choice that can be done after work is completed, then it might be titled: What Do I Do When I'm Done with My Assignment? In this case, whatever the curriculum or skill that the child was working on in his workbook or worksheet is applied and utilized through one of the activities. There is no such thing now as "I'm done, what do I do?" Students do not get *free time* when they complete an assignment. They work more with the skill.

Strategies & Activities Across the Curriculum

A Closer Look
A Real Life Classroom Example

Example Using Quotation Marks

I assigned the chart during independent work time. Students could do anything they wanted, but they had to be working with the curriculum of quotation marks.

Judy highlighted quotation marks in the book she was reading. Then she searched for the word 'SAID' and rewrote each sentence changing the word SAID.

"Mr. Ben said he saw the red Cardinal feeding another Cardinal," Josephine said to her mother.
"I bet he did," Mrs. Boo said to Josephine. "A male and female cardinal will stay together for life. Do you know what color the female cardinal is?"
"The female cardinal is light red. Mrs. Gremlin said she is light so that predators don't see her or her nest easily," said Josephine.
"That's Right. And do you know what color male cardinals are?" asked Mrs. Boo.
"Male cardinals are bright red," said Josephine.

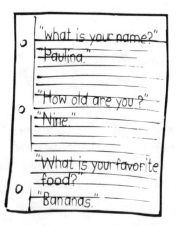

"What is your name?"
"Paulina."

"How old are you ?"
"Nine."

"What is your favorite food?"
"Bananas."

Rose conducted an interview with her friend. She used quotation marks in her writing.

John made a flipbook after reading *Frog and Toad*. Under the flaps he wrote sentences that each of the characters might say.

"My button is not square." "My button is not black."

"My button has 2 holes."

Example Using A Science Unit: The Ocean

While working with our ocean unit, I assigned the chart during independent work time. Students could do anything they wanted as long as they were working with the concepts from our science unit.

Philip used highlighting tape to mark all of the facts he found about the ocean. For some students using the highlighting tape might be the only thing they do. Students will actually turn in the book for the teacher to look through.

Trish filled in a sense web

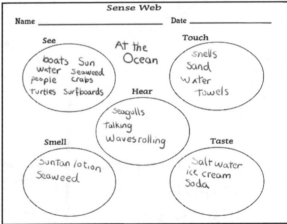

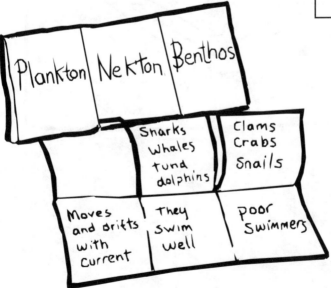

After highlighting all the facts, Alice took all of the information and organized it into a flipbook. Her flaps were labeled with the three levels of ocean life: Plankton, Nekton, and Benthos. Under each flap were facts and pictures of the different levels.

Strategies & Activities Across the Curriculum

You're Never at a Dead End

As educators, the ultimate goal we have for all of our students is that they begin to apply strategies on their own, that they learn how to be independent, strategic, successful learners. Students need to know exactly what to do when learning gets difficult. Students face dead ends all the time:

- I can't read the directions.
- I don't know what to do.
- I have nothing to write about.
- I can't figure out the answer.

They often do one of two things when faced with a dead end situation. Some students do nothing. They will just sit, look out the window, play with something in their desk. When asked if they need help their response is often, "No, I'm fine." They are very quiet and passive in their confusion. Other students do just the opposite. They are loud and active. These students often become behavior problems when they are faced with difficult tasks.

We need our students to know that there are no dead ends! Dead ends are not places to stop, but are places to make turns:

left turns,
right turns,
angled turns,
fly over it,
tunnel under it,
BUT DON'T
STOP!

As new strategies are learned, write them on signs and put them on posts. Students can refer to them anytime they are stuck.

For Younger Students

Take two or three cardboard wrapping tubes. Tape them together. Put the tubes onto a box with tape or push them into a hole you have cut out. As each new strategy is learned, write it on a colored piece of paper and attach it to the signpost. The goal is for students to use the signs on their own. Because the strategies are readily available for students to see EVERY DAY, they begin looking at the signs on their own. When first starting this, constantly bring students' attention to the signs, pointing out the strategies and activities at least three to four times per day. If you use colored paper, you can refer to the signs by color. For example, "Tom, try the blue sign. Laura, the red sign will help you with that question."

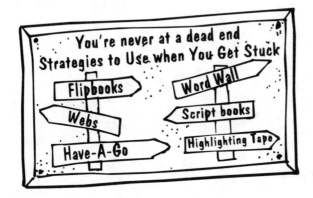

For Older Students

Follow the same idea as above but have students make the signpost and signs out of wood. They can paint and decorate the signs and hammer them to the post. This is a great activity to coordinate with the art teacher.

You can also make the signs and post with paper on a bulletin board or on the wall.

All of the strategies on the sign posts are explained in this book.

"The best teacher is not necessarily the one who possesses the most knowledge, but the one who most effectively enables his students to believe in their ability to learn."

Norma Cousins
The Heart and Wisdom of Teaching
compiled by Esther Wright

Part 4
Home/School Connection

Parents as Partners

As educators we understand that the ability to read and write are the significant achievements of the primary grades. We have seen significant changes in literacy instruction in our schools. We also recognize that children are more successful when a home/school partnership exists. So parents must be informed about instructional approaches and be given information to help them support literacy efforts at home. This section will look at the following two issues:

- Specific strategies and activities parents can do at home to support their children.

- Informing parents and creating a partnership through parent workshops.

One of the biggest concerns parents often have is exactly how to help their child. They need specific things to try at home. The first part of this section will offer some ideas that have been very successful.

"Parents are the first teachers children meet. They are also children's teachers for the longest periods. The success of the school literacy program frequently depends on the literacy environment at home."

Lesley Mandel Morrow
Literacy Development in the Early Years

Reading aloud is one of the most important ways parents can spend time with their children, but many times parents will say they want to do more. Below are some quotes that point out how very important this seemingly unimportant task can be. I usually send home a quote every other week with a parent newsletter.

"The best way to raise a reader is to read to that child — in the home and in the classroom."

Jim Trelease
The New Read-Aloud Handbook

"The single most important activity for building the knowledge required for eventual success in reading is reading aloud to children."

Report on The Commission on Reading
Becoming A Nation of Readers

"Children who come from homes in which storybook reading takes place have an educational advantage over those who do not."

Dorothy S. Strickland &
Lesley Mandel Morrow
*Emerging Literacy: Young Children Learn to
Read and Write*

You may have tangible wealth untold:
Caskets of jewels and coffers of gold.
Richer than I you can never be —
I had a mother who read to me.

Strickland Gillilan
The Reading Mother
from *Best Loved Poems of the
American People*

Comprehension and Language Development

After parents have read a story aloud or a child has completed an independent reading assignment, parents can ask their child to do a retelling of the read aloud or reading assignment. Retelling helps children review and organize the chapter and/or book. Parents can listen for the following:

- Does the retelling make sense?
- Is it organized in a sequence that *sounds right*?
- Has the child used the same story language and story pattern from the book?
- Does the parent have any questions that the child can clarify?

Parents can use the following prompts and suggestions:

- What was your favorite part? Why?
- What didn't you like? Why?
- What would you have done? Why?
- Predict what might happen next.

Stress to parents that this retelling is a catalyst for conversing about the book, not a *question and drill* about the reading. This is a time for parent and child to give opinions about characters, share feelings about issues in the book, etc. Parents can also give children a retelling about a book they are reading. This is a great way to role model the process. (See page 154 *Reading at Home*. That newsletter for parents includes the suggestions on this page.)

Chunking Homework

The parent letter and reproducible form on pages 140-141 help children and parents look at homework assignments and chunk them apart into smaller, more manageable pieces.

I usually send home a couple of sheets at a time in Monday's Home/School envelope (see pages 24-25). When parents need more forms they send in a note and their child brings extra forms home in their envelope. This form can be used for four separate assignments or to break up one assignment.

Chunk a Task into Smaller Parts

The parent and child need to look at the page of problems and divide the work into four smaller parts. Then, using the lines on the right side of the form, they write down the problems that need to be completed in four separate stages. As the child completes each section of work, he puts his initials in the box and then goes to see his parent(s). The parent(s) initials the space under the box and sets his child up for the next section.

Child's initial

Parent's initial

Take the 25 problems from the math book and chunk them into smaller tasks.

Managing Many Assignments

List each individual assignment on the right side. The top line is used to list the whole assignment, while the next two lines can be used to help break up each assignment.

All four boxes do not have to be used. Sometimes the assignment calls for only two or three boxes to be used. This strategy has helped parents make the homework more manageable for children. Also, parents have commented that their child does not keep calling out for them since he knows as soon as each piece is done he can get up and see mom/dad.

Child's initial

Parent's initial

Some students put a ✓ as they complete each piece.

Dear Parents:

The attached form will help you and your child chunk homework assignments into smaller, more manageable pieces. You can use this for up to four separate assignments, or to break one assignment into four separate tasks. Here are two examples to show how this might be used.

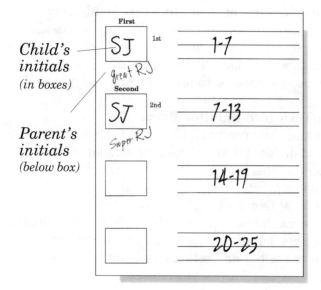

Child's initials
(in boxes)

Parent's initials
(below box)

Chunk a Task into Smaller Parts

Look at the assigned page of problems and think about dividing it into four parts. Then, using the lines on the right side of the form, write down the problems that need to be completed in four separate stages. As your child completes each section of work, he puts his initials in the box and then goes to you. You initial the space under the box and set your child up for the next section.

Take the 25 assigned problems and chunk them into smaller tasks.

Managing Many Assignments

To the right is an example of how to use the form when your child has several different homework assignments. List each individual assignment using the lines on the right. The top line is used to list the whole assignment, while the next two lines can be used to help break up each assignment. All four boxes do not have to be used. Sometimes the assignment calls for only two or three boxes to be used.

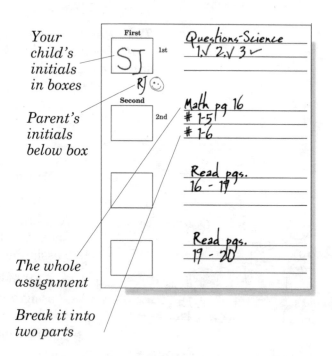

Your child's initials in boxes

Parent's initials below box

The whole assignment

Break it into two parts

These strategies may help make homework assignments more manageable for your child. Also, your child may stop calling out for you to help since he knows that as soon as each piece is done, he can get up and see you. Please do not hesitate to call if you have questions!

Sincerely,

First

1st

_____

_____

_____

Second

2nd

_____

_____

_____

Third

3rd

_____

_____

_____

Fourth

4th

_____

_____

_____

Calendar of Assignments and Responsibilities

Older students have many long term assignments that need to be completed throughout the year. Time management for long term assignments, even a week-long task, can be difficult for students to manage. If an assignment is not due tomorrow, many students feel they have an endless amount of time.

At the beginning of each month, send home a calendar of responsibilities and assignments for the month. This helps parents work with students so that they don't wait until the last minute and then get overwhelmed. Parents and children can use the same procedure as explained in chunking homework. Look at the assignment and break it into more manageable pieces (see page 139). Goals and time frames must also be established. Now, for example, if a child has three weeks to complete a report, then the following goals can be set and established with a specific time frame in mind:

On (date), all the resources (books, pictures, paper, etc.)
            needed for the report will be in hand

On (date), 2 paragraphs will be completed

On (date), 3 paragraphs will be completed

ETC.

Long term planning may be done at school as a part of the assignment. For example, the rough draft might be due in a week, the rough draft bibliography due in two weeks, etc. This helps students and parents take those benchmarks and really get down to the nitty gritty of how much will be done and when it needs to be completed.

MARCH						
SUN	MON	TUE	WED	THUR	FRI	SAT
	1 Bibliography is due	2	3	4	5	6
7	8	9 Outline due	10	11	12	13
14	15	16	17 St. Patrick's Day	18 Rough draph due	19	20
21	22	23	24	25	26	27
28 Palm Sunday	29 Final report due	30	31			

Spelling Strategy Folder

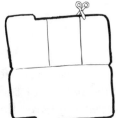

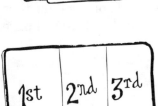

I recommend parents use this folder when helping their child study for spelling tests. It can also be used for individual words that children might be having difficulty with. Parents have said they spend 10 minutes a night using the folder to *play* with the most commonly misspelled words.

This activity is similar to Look, Cover, Write, Check found on pages 69-72. Have parents and children make this folder together. They will need a file folder and the reproducible boxes found on page 145. Cut the top of the file folder into three parts creating three flaps that can be lifted up.

On the outside of each flap write 1st, 2nd, 3rd.

Open the flaps. On the top of each of the flaps glue on the boxes found on page 145.

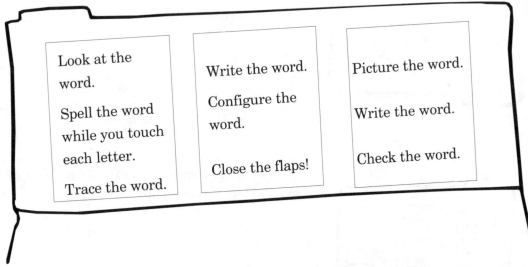

Look at the word.

Spell the word while you touch each letter.

Trace the word.

Write the word.

Configure the word.

Close the flaps!

Picture the word.

Write the word.

Check the word.

On the bottom inside of the folder, make two little cuts and insert paper clips through each slit. The left side is where children will clip on their list of words. The right side is where a blank piece of paper is put so students can practice the words.

Dear Parents:

Here is a strategy that I recommend using when helping your child study for spelling tests. It can also be used for individual words that your child might be having difficulty with. Spend about 10 minutes a night using this folder.

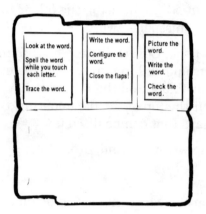

Make this folder together. You will need a file folder and the boxes found on the attached page. Cut the top of the file folder into three parts creating three flaps that can be lifted up. On the inside of the flaps that lift up, glue on the three boxes from the attatched page.

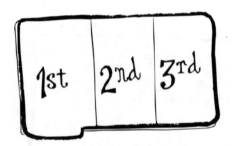

On the outside of each flap write 1st, 2nd, 3rd.

On the bottom inside of the folder, make two little cuts and insert paper clips through each slit. The left side is where your child will clip on his list of words. The right side is for a blank piece of paper so your child can practice the words.

Sincerely,

Look at the word.

Spell the word while you touch each letter.

Trace the word.

Write the word.

Configure the word.

Close the flaps!

Picture the word.

Write the word.

Check the word.

   mom dad

 able

 said because baby

How to Configure Words
When your child configures the word, he outlines around the letters. See examples to the right.

Reproducible

The beginning of this book discussed how important it is for students to make connections. When discussing how parents can help their children, point out how referencing certain events and familiar experiences can help children understand new concepts with more ease. Some specific suggestions are:

- Describe new concepts in relationship to something your child already knows.
- Brainstorm synonyms and antonyms for new vocabulary words.
- Draw pictures to clarify information.
- Find books, watch videos, and visit places that directly relate to what your child is learning in school.

Quick Books

Many parents have asked about flipbooks because their children talk about them at home. For homework one night, have students explain to their parents what flipbooks are and how to make them. The students need to bring back the flipbooks the next day with a quick note from their parents stating that the parent now knows what a flipbook is and how to make one.

Show parents how to make a Quick Book that can organize homework assignments as well as chores children need to do. Use any size piece of paper and just rip instead of cutting. The flaps may not be even in size or shape, but that is fine! The outside flaps are the homework assignment and/or chores, and under the flaps are the reinforcements and fun breaks. See the letter to parents on the following page. Send this letter home the day after you have assigned children to teach flipbooks to their parents.

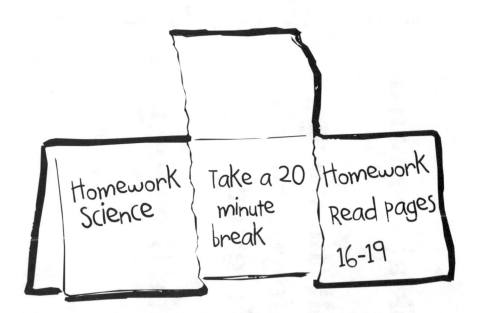

Dear Parents:

   Your child has taught you how to make a flipbook and has told you what we do with them in the classroom. Here is another suggestion called a Quick Book. Use any size piece of paper and just rip instead of cut. The flaps may not be even in size or shape, but that is fine! Write homework assignments or chores on the outside flaps and put reinforcements and fun breaks under the flaps. See two examples below.

                              Sincerely,

Outside of Quick Book

Inside of Quick Book

chore | Homework | chore

Get a hug | Take a 20 minute break | Give Sam a bone

Homework | chore | Get ready for bed

Outside of Quick Book

Get a snack | Hug from Mom | Mom will read a story

Inside of Quick Book

Parent Workshops

Helping Children Understand New Information

Parent evenings/workshops are great ways to build successful home/school connections. These evenings give parents opportunities to ask questions and share. They also inform parents about:

- Instructional Approaches
- Materials
- Philosophies

They encourage parents to support reading and writing at home, and give specific suggestions for doing so.

Tips

Tips for successful parent evenings

Informal and relaxed

Greet parents at the door. It's always such a great feeling when I come home from a day at work and my family is at the door saying hello and asking about my day. I've gone to workshops and been greeted with a big smile and hello right at the entrance. This greeting sets the tone for feeling welcome, comfortable, and excited to be there.

Play soft music in the background to create a relaxed and informal atmosphere. Give parents time to visit with each other. I start the evenings 5-10 minutes late so parents have time to talk with each other. Coffee and snacks are available. My students make the snacks, brownies, and cupcakes during the school day.

Time frames

Schedule the meeting for 1½ hours. I usually have at least two parent evenings each year. Schedule each meeting for a different time, that way all parents will hopefully have one time that is more convienient for them. Suggested times can be:

      5:30-7:00   6:00-7:30   6:30-8:00

Provide child care

The biggest problem parents vocalized was needing babysitters for their children. Providing child care where the meeting takes place will give more parents the opportunity to come. Who can babysit?

- School board members
- Teachers who are not involved in the evening
- Parents from years past
- Parents from years to come
- Older students in the school

Begin and end with a story/poem

What better way to model the love of reading!

Give parents the date and time for the next meeting before they leave.

Here are some suggestions to get the word out about the workshops.

School Calendar

If you have a school calendar, list workshops in the upcoming events the month before, as well as the month it occurs.

Article in School Newspaper

If you have a school newspaper, write an article the month before, as well as the month you plan on having the meeting. Include pictures of students helping you get ready.

Local Papers

Put articles in your local newspapers. Include pictures of your students writing out invitations for the workshops and making the refreshments.

Invitations

Two kinds of invitations go home. Students make personal invitations for their parents or guardians. They take these home themselves. Get your students excited about having their family come to school. Some of my parents told me they came because their child kept talking about it and asking them to go. The other invitation is made by the teacher and gets sent through the mail to parents.

Personal Phone Calls

Have a phone call relay. Call two parents and have them call two, and so on. I make contact with a parent that I know will come and get very excited about the idea. He/she is a great resource to have phoning other parents. I also call parents who I know will have a difficult time coming, so I try to help in any way and encourage them to come.

Follow-up Articles

After each evening, have follow up articles and messages in the local newspapers, school newspapers, and school calendars.

Word of Mouth

Good news travels fast. You may not have a large group the first evening, but watch each meeting grow.

Handouts

On pages 152 and 154, you will find handouts that can be used to give parents ideas about reading and writing at home with their children.

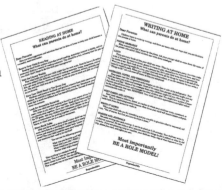

A Closer Look

A Real Life Classroom Example

Below are some pictures from parent workshops that Beth Richards, a first grade teacher in New Hampshire, and I organized.

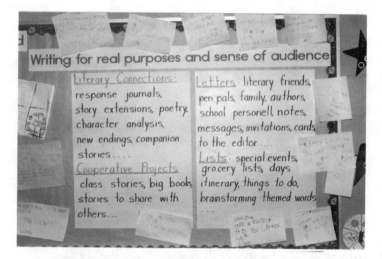

We set up bulletin boards that displayed posters with information about the reading process and writing process. All around these posters are samples of children's writing that have been done at school and at home.

Explaining print concepts to parents.

This was a bulletin board we set up at the writing workshop to help explain some concerns about inventive spelling.

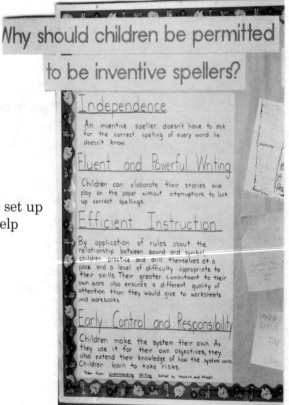

Instructional materials were available so parents could interact with them. On display were big books, storyboards, masks, puppets, flannel boards, and a wealth of quality children's literature.

Instructional methods such as guided reading, shared reading, language experience stories, and retelling strategies were discussed.

WRITING AT HOME
What can parents do at home?

Dear Parents:

Children learn to write by writing, and there are many different ways that you can facilitate this process at home.

PHONE MESSAGES

Keep a pencil and pad of paper by the phone. Ask your younger child to write down the name of the person who called. Older children can write down messages.

LISTS

There are many kinds of lists your child can write. When he is planning a party, have him make a list of friends he wants to invite, games he wants to play, decorations he wants to have, and food he wants to eat. Each week as you write a grocery list, have your child write his own grocery list. When you are getting ready for a trip, your child can write all the things he wants to do and all the items he needs to pack. When your child gets home from school, or on the weekend, he can write a "Things to Do" list and cross off items as they are completed.

MESSAGES, NOTES, AND REMINDERS

Keep paper near the refrigerator and a magnet on the door or side of the refrigerator. Your child can leave you notes and messages. Some of the notes from younger children might just say "Hi Mom and Dad." Some of the messages from older children might tell you where they are. Parents should leave notes and messages for their children also! You might have a piece of paper on the refrigerator that says, REMINDER. Your child can write appointments and after school commitments under it.

POST CARDS AND LETTERS

Each week choose a relative, friend, or teacher to whom your child can write a postcard or letter. This is a motivating activity because often times your child will receive letters and post-cards back from the person he wrote to.

WRITE IT DOWN!

When your child asks you for something and you are able to give him what he requested, tell him, "Yes, of course, but first you have to write it down."

DIARIES AND JOURNALS

Set aside writing time each evening. It can be as short as 5-10 minutes. Your child can write in a diary or a journal. He can write or draw pictures about the things he did in school, or what he did at home. If you are planning a trip or vacation, your child can keep a log of what happened on the trip, places you went, and sights you saw.

Most importantly
BE A ROLE MODEL!

A Closer Look
A Real Life Home Example

Writing at Home

Some parents sent in the following samples and ideas of what they were doing at home with their children.

Children can write their own grocery lists while parents write the family list. One parent said after her child (Stacie) wrote the list she was allowed to circle her two favorite things and they would buy them. Below is Stacie's grocery list.

chocolate bar
waffles
candy corn
fruit roll ups
ice cream
popcorn

Another parent has her child write down things she wants. Christine writes:

Mom and Dad can I have a snack.

She realizes she forgot something and rewrites:

Dad and Mom can I have a snack please.

READING AT HOME
What can parents do at home?

Dear Parents:

Here are some suggestions and activities that can be done at home to help your child become a successful, motivated reader.

Read to Your Child Every Day

Reading aloud builds positive attitudes toward reading, stimulates interest in books, and exposes your child to a variety of reading materials. This should be a fun, relaxing time for you and your child. Don't forget to do this with your teenagers too!

Visit the Library Weekly

Plan what books you and your child might like for each week. Does he have a favorite author or a favorite subject? Get different varieties of reading materials: books, magazines, and newspapers. Also, get many different varieties of topics: mysteries, nonfiction, science, animals, poems, rhymes, etc. You and your child may go to the library with no plan in mind and pick out what interests you as you browse.

Have Your Child Read to You Every Day

Children need positive feedback and genuine interest from their parents about their reading abilities. Be excited to hear your child read to you every day. Sometimes your child may choose a book that is much too difficult but has beautiful pictures. Instead of reading, have him tell you about the pictures.

Look for Accessible Materials

Help your child see that reading is found in every aspect of our lives. Have your child help you read a recipe as you cook or bake together. Read all the boxes and labels with your younger child as you grocery shop together. Have your older child figure out one TV show to watch by looking in the TV guide. Ask your child to find a telephone number in the phone book, look at directions to a game or instructions for putting together a model. Have your child find signs as you travel somewhere, or when you are in a mall or restaurant.

Share Book Talks

After you have read a story aloud or your child has completed an independent reading assignment, have him do a retelling of the read aloud or reading assignment. Retelling helps children review and organize the chapter and/or book. Listen for the following: Does the retelling make sense? Has your child used the same story language and story pattern from the book? Do you have any questions that need to be clarified?

You can use the following prompts and suggestions:

What was you favorite part? Why?
What didn't you like? Why?
What would you have done? Why?
Predict what might happen next.

This retelling is a catalyst for conversing about the book, not a "question and drill" about the reading. This is a time for you and your child to give opinions about characters and share feelings about issues in the book. You can also give your child a retelling about a book you are reading. This is a great way to role model that process.

Most Importantly
BE A ROLE MODEL!

Resources

Suggested Professional Reading

On the following pages are some suggested professional reading. There is a wealth of resources available to teachers. This list gives only a small number of suggestions based on all the resources available.

Assessment

Beaver, Teri. *The Author's Profile*. York, ME: Stenhouse Publishers, 1998.

Clay, Marie M. *The Early Detection of Reading Difficulties*. Portsmouth, NH: Heinemann, 1979.

Clay, Marie M. *An Observation Survey*. Portsmouth, NH: Heinemann, 1993.

Drummond, Mary Jane. *Learning to See*. York, ME: Stenhouse Publishers, 1994.

Power, Brenda Miller. *Taking Note*. York, ME: Stenhouse Publishers, 1996.

Rhodes, Lynn K. *Literacy Assessment*. York, ME: Stenhouse Publishers, 1993.

Brain Based Learning

Jensen, Eric. *Brain Compatible Strategies*. Del Mar, CA: Turning Point Publishing, 1997.

Jensen, Eric. *Introduction to Brain Compatible Learning*. San Diego, CA: The Brain Store, 1998.

Jensen, Eric. *Introduction to a Brain in Mind*. Alexandria, VA: ASCD, 1998.

Sylvester, Robert. *A Celebration of Neurons*. Alexandria, VA: ASCD, 1995.

Wolfe, Pat. *Mind, Memory, and Learning: Translating Brain Research to Classroom Practice*. Napa, CA: Patricia Wolfe, 1996.

Miscellaneous

Bromely, Karen, and Linda Irwin-De Vitis, et. al. *Graphic Organizers*. New York, NY: Scholastic, 1995.

Feldman, Jean R. *Wonderful Rooms Where Children Can Bloom*! Peterborough, NH: Crystal Springs Books, 1997.

Fisher, Bobbi. *Thinking and Learning Together*. Portsmouth, NH: Heinemann, 1995.

Ingraham, Phoebe Bell. *Creating and Managing Learning Centers*. Peterborough, NH: Crystal Springs Books, 1997.

Payne, Ruby K., Ph.D. *Poverty*. Baytown, TX: RFT Publishing, 1995.

Moline, Steve. *I See What You Mean*. York, ME: Stenhouse Publishers, 1995.

Routman, Regie. *Literacy at the Crossroads*. Portsmouth, NH: Heinemann, 1996.

Multiage and Looping

Forsten, Char, Jim Grant, Bob Johnson, and Irv Richardson. *Looping Q&A: 72 Answers to Your Most Pressing Questions*. Peterborough, NH: Crystal Springs Books, 1997.

Grant, Jim. *The Multiage Handbook*. Peterborough, NH: Crystal Springs Books, 1996.

Grant, Jim, Bob Johnson, and Irv Richardson. *Our Best Advice: The Multiage Problem Solving Handbook*. Peterborough, NH: Crystal Springs Books, 1996.

Grant, Jim, Bob Johnson, and Irv Richardson. *Multiage Q&A: 101 Practical Answers to Your Most Pressing Questions*. Peterborough, NH: Crystal Springs Books, 1995.

Rathbone, Charles. *Multiage Portraits: Teaching and Learning in Mixed-Age Classrooms*. Peterborough, NH: Crystal Springs Books, 1993.

Reading

Dorn, Linda and Cathy French, et al. *Apprenticeship in Literacy*. York, ME: Stenhouse, 1998.

Cunningham, Patricia M. and Dorothy P. Hall. *Making Words*. Torrance, CA: Good Apple, 1994.

Cunningham, Patricia. *Phonics They Use*. New York, NY: Harper Collins, 1995.

Einstein, Carol. *Be Your Own Reading Specialist*. Rosemont, NJ: Modern Learning Press, 1997.

Fitzpatrick, Jo. *Phonemic Awareness*. Cypress, CA: Creative Teaching Press, 1997.

Fountas, Irene C., and Gay Su Pinnell. *Guided Reading*. Portsmouth, NH: Heinemann, 1996.

Pavelka, Patricia. *Making the Connection: Learning Skills Through Literature* (K-2). Peterborough, NH: Crystal Springs Books, 1995.

Pavelka, Patricia. *Making the Connection: Learning Skills Through Literature* (3-6). Peterborough, NH: Crystal Springs Books, 1997.

Spelling

Bear, Donald R. and Shane Templeton. *Words Their Way*. Columbus, OH: Prentice Hall, 1996.

Gentry, Richard J. *My Kid Can't Spell*. Portsmouth, NH: Heinemann, 1997.

Gentry, Richard J. *Spel . . . Is a Four-Letter Word*. Portsmouth, NH: Heinemann, 1987.

Gentry, Richard J., and Jean Wallace Gillet. *Teaching Kids to Spell*. Portsmouth, NH: Heinemann, 1993.

Hong, Min, and Patsy Stafford. *Spelling Strategies That Work*. New York, NY: Scholastic, 1997.

Hughes, Margaret, and Dennis Searle. *The Violent E and Other Tricky Sounds*. York, ME: Stenhouse Publishers, 1997.

Students with Learning Difficulties

Goodman, Gretchen. *I Can Learn!* Peterborough, NH: Crystal Springs Books, 1995.

Goodman, Gretchen. *More I Can Learn!* Peterborough, NH: Crystal Springs Books, 1998.

Grant, Jim, and Irv Richardson. *The Retention/Promotion Checklist*. Peterborough, NH: Crystal Springs, 1998.

Rief, Sandra F. *How to Reach and Teach ADD/ADHD Children*. West Nyack, NY: The Center for Applied Research in Education, 1993.

Writing

Calkins, Lucy McCormick. *The Art of Teaching Writing*. Portsmouth, NH: Heinemann, 1994.

Graves, Donald H. *A Fresh Look at Writing*. Portsmouth, NH: Heinemann, 1994.

Harvey, Stephanie. *Nonfiction Matters*. York, ME: Stenhouse, 1998.

Merrilees, Cindy, and Pamela Haack. *Write On Target*. Peterborough, NH: Crystal Springs Books, 1990.

Robb, Laura. *Reading & Writing Conferences*. New York, NY: Scholastic, 1998.

Short, Kathy G. *Creating Classrooms for Authors and Inquirers*. Portsmouth, NH: Heinemann, 1996.

Sunflower, Cherilyn. *75 Creative Ways to Publish Students' Writing*. New York, NY: Scholastic, 1993.